PREFACE

As a nation we look to our founding fathers with reverence and awe. The Declaration of Independence and Constitution are quasi-religious documents to many Americans. These inspired writings were not born out of a vacuum; they were influenced by the works of philosophers and statesmen that had seen the evils in government in their day and advocated for a better way.

In our increasingly globalized world, we are confronted with a number of world views and ideologies that often directly conflict with our own value system. While free societies and free markets have been proven to bring greater happiness, innovation and prosperity than closed systems, these models continue to be challenged by those who would choose a path of planned economies and limited personal liberties. In the age of moral relativisms we find ourselves less and less equipped to advocate for those values for which generations before pledged their "…lives, fortunes and sacred honor."

In our day of increasing globalism and routine attacks on personal liberty, it is ever more important to prepare ourselves and the rising generation to stand-up in defense of our common values.

This short work attempts to collect and organize quotes and commentary by those philosophers that would have influenced and inspired our founding fathers. While there are a few quotes that post-date the drafting of our constitution — seminal observations on the freedoms established by that document by Tocqueville and Mill — the vast majority are from works that would have been read by those great men.

As we come to appreciate the philosophical underpinnings of the policy decisions made in drafting the US Constitution, we will be better armed with arguments to defend liberty. The authors quoted could only look forward in hope for a better and more enlightened day. It is my hope that many will read the words of these great statesmen and find in them the inspiration to defend the cause of freedom.

Gabriel C. Lajeunesse
Kabul, Afghanistan
September, 2012

INTRODUCTION

The text that follows is an arrangement of quotes grouped into eight chapters, further collated under sub-headers by rough themes. At the end of each sub-heading are questions meant to generate discussion or thought regarding the relevance of the preceding material. The chapters conclude with proposed exercises, to turn the learning achieved into action.

This work has limited entertainment value. Much of the material presented contemplates significant questions regarding the purpose of life and society. It is not designed to be read through as a novel. Rather, it is meant for in depth study, meditation and discussion, as personal or family time permits. Reading a quote at a time, or a section at a time, will allow for greater appreciation for the arguments made.

Using a study journal to record personal impressions may increase the value of individual study.

CONTENTS

1. The Education of a Free Society   1

2. The Rights of Man   7

3. Peace – The Purpose of Government   29

4. Leadership in Government   41

5. Constitutional Government   51

6. The Natural Law and the Laws of Man   65

7. On Warfare   75

8. On Tyranny   97

Appendix A. Virginia Declaration of Rights 109
Appendix B.   US Constitutional   115

REFERENCED WORKS

Aquinas, Thomas, *Summa Theologica*
Aristotle, *Politics*
Cicero, *Political Speeches*
Epictetus, *Discourses; Enchiridion*
Grotius, Hugo, *On the Law of War and Peace*
Hobbes, Thomas, *Leviathian*
Kant, Immanuel, *Perpetual Peace; Theory and Practice*
Locke, John, *Two Treatises on Government*
Machiavelli, Niccolo, *The Prince; Discourses*
Montesquieu, Baron de, *The Spirit of Laws*
Mill, John Stuart, *On Liberty*
Paine, Thomas, *Common Sense*
Plato, *The Republic*
Rousseau, Jean Jacques, *On the Social Contract*
Thucydides, *Peloponnesian War*
de Tocqueville, Alexis *Democracy in America*
Trechard, John and Gordon, Thomas, *Cato's Letters*
Wilson, James, *Lectures on Law*

Chapter 1: The Education of a Free Society

Throughout human history, liberty – our God given heritage – has been usurped by strongmen who imposed their will, through force of arms or internal political faction, upon the people they governed. The strongest bulwark against oppression is the education of society, so that the innate love of freedom within each citizen is strengthened as understanding increases. Thus, those who would oppress must not simply conquer through military means or political intrigue, but must utterly destroy the educated, individual will of each citizen it hopes to subject. Families, teachers and civil organizations protect and preserve freedoms as they work to instill a love of constitutional government in those they have stewardship over.

I. To preserve constitutional government we must love it.

"...virtue is a self-renunciation of which is ever arduous and painful. This virtue may be defined as the love of laws and of our country. As such love requires a constant preference of public to private interests, it is the source of all private virtue; for they are nothing more than this very preference itself. This love is peculiar to democracies. In these alone is government entrusted to private citizens. Now government is like everything else: to preserve it we must love it...Everything therefore, depends on establishing this love in a republic; and to inspire it ought to be the principal business of education: but the surest way of instilling it into children is for parents to set the example. People have it generally in their power to communicate their ideas to their children; but they are

still better able to transfuse their passions...It is not the young people that degenerate; they are not spoiled till those of mature age are already sunk into corruption." (Montesquieu)

Questions for Discussion:
1. How do we become more inclined to put public interest ahead of our own private interests?
2. What can we do as individuals and community leaders to instill a love of laws and of our country in ourselves and to those we interact with?

II. The importance of inspiring virtue through laws, education, media and entertainment

"..in the making of laws, the pleasures and fears of

particular men, being the great engines by which they are to governed, must be consulted. Vice must be rendered detestable and dangerous, virtue amiable and advantageous. Their shame and emulation must be raised: their private profit and glory, peril and infamy, laid before them." (Trenchard)

"[this law]…is not engraved on marble or bronze, but in the hearts of citizens. It is the true constitution of the state. Everyday it takes on new forces. When other laws grow old and die away, it revives and replaces them, preserves a people in the spirit of its institution and imperceptibly substitutes the force of habit for that of authority. I am speaking of mores, customs, and especially of opinion, a part of the law unknown to our political theorists but one on which depends the success of all the others; a part with which the great legislator secretly occupies himself, though he seems to confine himself to the particular regulations that are merely the aching of the vault, whereas mores, slower to arise, form in the end its immovable keystone." (Rousseau)

"Children cannot distinguish between what is allegory and what isn't, and opinions formed at that age are usually difficult to eradicate or change; we should therefore surely regard it as the utmost importance that the first stories they hear shall aim at encouraging the highest excellence of character." (Plato)

"We shall thus prevent our guardians being brought up among representations of what is evil and so day by day and little by little, by grazing widely as it were in an unhealthy pasture, insensibly doing themselves a cumulative psychological damage that is very serious." (Plato)

"if a state is to be on the right lines, every possible step must be taken to prevent anyone, young or old, either saying or being told, whether in poetry or prose, that god, being good, can cause harm or evil to any man. To say so would be sinful, inexpedient, and inconsistent. God is the cause, not of all things, but only of good." (Plato)

"But it is not enough just to hand out the sort of maxims which warn him off evil things and summon him to the good. No, they must be fixed in his mind, pressed in, and rammed home. And they must be kept fresh in memory in all sorts of ways: sometimes in a moral maxim, sometimes in a parable, sometimes by an analogy, sometimes by a live example, an epigram, or a proverb; they must be carved on rings, painted in pictures, inscribed on prizes, and presented in any other way that a child of his age enjoys, so that they are always before his mind, even when he is doing something else." (Erasmus)

Happiness is the centre, to which men and nations are attracted: it is, therefore, the duty of a nation to consult its happiness. In order to do this, it is necessary that the nation be instructed to search for happiness where happiness is to be found. The impressions that are made first, sink deepest; they frequently continue through life. That seed, which is sown in the tender minds of youth, will produce abundance of good, or abundance of evil. The education of youth, therefore, is of prime importance to the happiness of the state. The arts, the sciences, philosophy, virtue, and religion, all contribute to the happiness, all, therefore, ought to receive the encouragement, of the nation. In this manner, publick and private felicity will go hand in hand, and mutually assist each other in their progress." (Wilson)

Questions for Discussion:

1. Trenchard says of our laws, "Vice must be rendered detestable and dangerous, virtue amiable and advantageous." How is this done? What should we expect of our legislators? Do we have a role as private citizens?
2. What is the relationship between the books, movies and other media influences we consume and our dedication to the cause of liberty?

End of Chapter Exercises

1. Make a list of traditions, celebrations, or remembrance events you will participate in to periodically refocus on the values of constitutional government and freedom.
2. Develop a collection of books, articles and other media which inspire excellence of character. Make a point to avoid media and other influences which would weaken us by "grazing widely as it were in an unhealthy pasture."

Chapter 2. The Rights of Man

Protection of liberty and individual freedoms are essential functions of government. Prosperity, development, invention, and innovation will flourish more fully where freedom is established. Personal growth and improvement is possible only where freedom of choice is respected and individuals can learn through their own experience. "...We hold these truths to be self-evident, that all men are created equal, that they are endowed by their Creator with certain unalienable Rights, that among these are Life, Liberty and the pursuit of Happiness. — That to secure these rights, Governments are instituted among Men, deriving their just powers from the consent of the governed..." Declaration of Independence.

I. Free Societies in General

"...as we love our religion, and the author of it, we ought to love and preserve our liberties." (Trenchard)

"The two great laws of human society, from whence all the rest derive their course and obligation, are those of equity and self-preservation. By the first all men are bound alike to not hurt one another; by the second all men have a right alike to defend themselves." (Trenchard)

"The rights of men must be held sacred, however great the cost of sacrifice may be to those in power. Here one cannot go halfway, cooking up hybrid, pragmatically-conditioned rights (which are somewhere between the right and the expedient); instead, all politics must bend its knee before morality, and by so doing it can hope to reach, though but gradually, the stage where it will shine in light perpetual." (Kant)

"Both the love of man and the respect for the rights of man are our duty; the former is only conditional, while the later is unconditional, absolutely imperative duty, a duty that one must be completely certain of not having transgressed, if one is to be able to enjoy the sweet sense of having done right." (Kant)

"All men are born free; liberty is a gift which they receive from God himself; nor can they alienate the same by consent, though possibly they may forfeit it by their crimes. No man has power of his own life, or to dispose of his own religion, and cannot consequently transfer the power to any other body else. Much less can he give away the lives, liberties, religion or acquired property of his posterity, which will be born as free as he himself was born and can never be bound by his wicked and ridiculous bargain. The right of the magistrate arises only from the private right of men to defend themselves, to repel injuries and to punish those who committed them: That right being conveyed by the society to their public representative, he can execute the same no further than the benefit and security of that society requires he should." (Trenchard)

"In civil society, previously to the institution of civil government, all men are equal. Of one blood all nations are made; from one source the whole human race has sprung. When we say, that all men are equal; we mean not to apply this equality to their virtues, their talents, their dispositions, or their acquirements. In all these respects, there is, and it is fit for the great purposes of society that there should be, great inequality among men. In the moral and political as well as in the natural world, diversity forms an important part of beauty; and as of beauty, so of utility likewise. That social happiness, which arises from the friendly intercourse of good offices, could not be enjoyed, unless men were so framed and so disposed, as mutually to afford and to stand in need of service and assistance. Hence the necessity not only of great variety, but even of great inequality in the talents of men, bodily as well as mental. Society supposes mutual dependence: mutual dependence supposes mutual wants: all the social exercises and enjoyments may be reduced to two heads—that of giving, and that of receiving: but these imply different aptitudes to give and to receive….But however great the variety and inequality of men may be with regard to virtue, talents, taste, and acquirements… there is an equality in rights and in obligations…The natural rights and duties of man belong equally to all." (Wilson)

"Americans of all ages, all conditions, and all dispositions, constantly form associations. They have not only commercial and manufacturing companies, in which all take part, but associations of a thousand other kinds - religious, moral, serious, futile, extensive, or restricted, enormous or diminutive. The Americans make associations to give entertainments, to found establishments for education, to build inns, to construct churches, to diffuse books, to send missionaries to the antipodes; and in this manner they found hospitals, prisons, and schools. If it be proposed to advance some truth, or to foster some feeling by the encouragement of a great example, they form a society. Wherever, at the head of some new undertaking, you see the government in France, or a man of rank in England, in the United States you will be sure to find an association. I met with several kinds of associations in America, of which I confess I had no previous notion; and I have often admired the extreme skill with which the inhabitants of the United States succeed in proposing a common object to the exertions of a great many men, and in getting them voluntarily to pursue it...Nothing, in my opinion, is more deserving of our attention than the intellectual and moral associations of America...If men are to remain civilized, or to become so, the art of associating together must grow and improve in the same ratio in which the equality of conditions is increased." (Tocqueville)

In America the principle of the sovereignty of the people is not either barren or concealed, as it is with some other nations; it is recognized by the customs and proclaimed by the laws; it spreads freely, and arrives without impediment at its most remote consequences. If there be a country in the world where the doctrine of the sovereignty of the people can be fairly appreciated, where it can be studied in its application to the affairs of society, and where its dangers and its advantages may be foreseen, that country is assuredly America. (Tocqueville)

Question for Discussion:
  1. Why must individual rights be held

sacrosanct? What blessing flow to us as individuals and societies as these rights are protected?

II. Freedom of Conscience

"First...the care of souls is not committed to the civil magistrate because...it appears not that God has ever given any such authority to one man over another as to compel anyone in his religion...In the second place, the care of the souls cannot belong to the civil magistrate, because his power consists only in outward force; but true and saving religion consists in the inward persuasion of the mind, without which nothing can be acceptable to God...In the third place...in the variety and contradiction of opinions in religion, wherein princes of the world are as much divided as in their secular interests, the narrow way would be much strained, one country alone would be right, and all the rest of the world would be put under obligation of following their princes in the ways that lead to destruction..." (Locke)

"Philosophic liberty consists in the free exercise of the will; or at least, if we must speak agreeable to all systems, in the opinion that we have the free exercise of our will. Political liberty consists in security, or at least in the opinion that we enjoy security." (Montesquieu)

"Every man's religion is his own; nor can the religion of any man, of what nature or figure soever, be the religion of another man, unless he also chooses it which action utterly excludes all force, power or government.

Religion can never come without conviction, nor can conviction come from civil authority, religion, which is the fear of God, cannot be subject to power, which is the fear of man." (Trenchard)

"Almighty God, the great author of our nature, and of all things, who has the heavens for his throne and the earth for his footstool, is raised far above the reach of our kindness, our malice or our flattery. He derives infinite happiness from his own infinite perfections; nor can any frail power or action of ours lessen or improve it; religion therefore, from which he can reap no advantage, was instituted by him for the sake of men, as the best means and the strongest motive to their own happiness, and mutual happiness; and by it men are taught and animated to be useful, assisting, forgiving, kind and merciful to one another.   But to hurt, calumniate, or hate one another, for his sake, and in defense of any religion, is a flat contradiction to his religion, and an open defiance of the author of religion: And to quarrel about belief and opinions, which do not immediately and necessarily produce practical virtue and social duties, is equally wicked and absurd. This is to be wicked in behalf of righteousness, and to be cruel out of piety. A religion which begets selfishness and partiality only to a few, and its own followers, and which inspires hatred and outrage towards all the rest of the world, can never be the religion of the merciful an impartial maker and judge of the world." (Trenchard)

"Both the spiritual power and the secular power derive from God's power. And so the secular power is subject to the spiritual power insofar as God has subjected the former to the later, namely, in matters pertaining to the salvation of souls. And so we should obey the spiritual power rather than the secular power in such matters. But in matters pertaining to civic welfare, we should obey the secular power rather than the spiritual power...Render to Caesar the things that are Caesar's." (Aquinas)

"When...men attack religious opinions, they obey the dictates of their passions to the prejudice of their interests. Despotism may govern without faith, but liberty cannot. Religion is much more necessary in the republic which they set forth in glowing colors than in the monarchy which they attack; and it is more needed in democratic republics than in any others. How is it possible that society should escape destruction if the moral tie be not strengthened in proportion as the political tie is relaxed? and what can be done with a people which is its own master, if it be not submissive to the Divinity?" (Tocqueville)

Question for Discussion:
1. What blessings come to a society through freedom of conscience and free exercise of religion?

III. Property Rights

"Where liberty is thoroughly established, and its laws equally established, and every man will find his account in doing as he would be done unto, and no man will take from another what he would not part

himself: Honor and advantage will follow the upright, punishment overtake the oppressor. The property of the poor will be as sacred as the privileges of the prince, and the law will be the only bulwark of both. Every man's honest industry and useful talents, while they are employed for the public, will be employed for himself, and while he serves himself he will serve the public: public and private interest will secure each other; all will cheerfully give a part to secure the whole and be brave to defend it." (Trenchard)

"The public revenues are a portion that each subject gives of his property, in order to secure or enjoy the remainder. To fix these revenues in a proper manner, regard should be had both to the necessities of the state, and to those of the subject. The real wants of the people ought never to give way to imaginary wants of the state." (Montesquieu)

"The effect of wealth in a country is to inspire every heart with ambition: that of poverty is to give birth to despair. The former is excited by labor, the latter is soothed by indolence. Nature is just to all mankind, and repays them for their industry: she renders them industrious by annexing rewards in proportion to their labor. But if an arbitrary prince should attempt to deprive the people of nature's bounty, they would fall into a disrelish of industry; and then indolence and inaction must be their only happiness." (Montesquieu)

"It was judged that every man had an equal share of that which was necessary for nature, that whatsoever was necessary for nature ought not to be taxed; that to this succeeded the useful, which ought to be taxed, but less than the superfluous, and that the largeness of the taxes on what was superfluous prevented superfluity." (Montesquieu)

"...liberty is, to be free from restraint and violence from others; which cannot be, where there is no law: but freedom is not a liberty for every man to do what he lists: but a liberty to dispose, and order as he lists, his person, action, possessions, and his whole property, within the allowance of those laws under which he is, and therein not to be subject to the arbitrary will of another, but freely follow his own." (Locke)

"Where there is liberty, there are encouragements to

labor, because people labor for themselves; and no one can take from them the acquisitions which they make by their labor: There will be the greatest numbers of people, because they find employment and protection; there will be the greatest stocks, because most is to be got, and easier to be got, and safest when it is got; and those stock will be always increasing by a new accession of money acquired elsewhere, where there is no security of enjoying it; there people will be able to work cheapest, because less taxes will be put upon their work, and upon the necessaries which must support them whilst they are about it: There people will dare to own their being rich; there will be most people bred up to trade, and trade and traders will be most respected; and there the interests of money will be lower, and the security of possessing it greater, than it can ever be in tyrannical governments, where life and property and all things must depend upon the humor of a prince, the caprice of a minister, or the demand of a harlot." (Trenchard)

"Men will not spontaneously toil and labor but for their own advantage, for their pleasure or their profit, and to obtain something which they want or desire, and which, for the most part, is not to be obtained but by force or consent." (Trenchard)

"...as happiness is the effect of independency, and independency the effect of property, so certain property is the effect of liberty alone, and can only be secured by the laws of liberty, laws which are made by consent, and cannot be repealed without it. All these blessings, therefore, are only the gifts and consequences of liberty, and only to be found in free countries, where power is fixed on one side, and property is secured on the other, where the one cannot break bound without check, penalties, or forfeiture, nor the other suffer diminution without redress, where the people have no masters but the laws, and such as the laws appoint; where both laws and magistracy are formed by the people or their deputies; and no demands are made upon them, but what are made by the law, and they know to a penny what to pay before it is asked; where they that exact from them more that the law allows, are punishable by the laws and where legislators are equally bound by their own acts, equally involved in the consequences." (Trenchard)

"How can a man or people seize a vast amount of territory and deprive the entire human race of it except by a punishable usurpation, since this seizure deprives all other men of shelter and sustenance that nature gives them in common?" (Rousseau)

"..we know God hath not left one man so to the mercy of another, that he may starve him if he please: God the Lord and Father of all has given no one of his children such property in peculiar portion of things off this world, but that he has given his needy brother a right to the surplus of his goods; so that it cannot be justly denied him when his pressing want calls for it; and therefore no man could ever have a just power over the life of another by the right of property in land or possessions; since it would always be a sin, in any man of estate, to let his brother perish for want of affording him relief out of his plenty. As justice gives every man a title to the product of his honest industry, and the fair acquisition of his ancestors descended to him, so charity gives every man a title to so much out of another's plenty as will keep him from extreme want where he has no means to subsist otherwise..." (Locke)

"True is it that when a democracy is founded on commerce, private people may acquire vast riches without a corruption of morals. This is because the spirit of commerce is naturally attended with that of frugality, economy, moderation, labor prudence, tranquility, order and rule. So long as this spirit subsists, the riches it produces have no bad effect." (Montesquieu)

"True and impartial liberty is therefore the right of every man to pursue the natural, reasonable, and religious dictates of his own mind: to think what he will, and act as he thinks, provided he acts not to the prejudice of another; to spend his own money himself, and lay out the produce of his labor his own way, and to labor for his own pleasure and profit, and not for others who are idle, and would live and riot by pillaging and oppressing him, and those that are like him." (Trenchard)

"What if the poor, on the ground of their being a majority, proceed to divide among themselves the possessions of the wealthy — will not this be unjust? 'No by heaven', someone may reply, 'it has been justly decreed so by the sovereign body.' But if this is not the extreme of injustice, what is? Whenever a majority takes everything and divides among its members the possessions of a minority, that majority is obviously ruining the city. But goodness does not ruin whatever possesses it, nor can justice be such as to ruin a city. It is therefore clear that a law of this kind cannot be possibly be just." (Aristotle)

"...the policy nowadays followed by the demagogues should be avoided. It is their habit to distribute any surpluses among the people; and the people, in the very act of taking them, ask for the same again. To help the poor in this way is like trying to fill a leaky jar." (Aristotle)

"The morals and the intelligence of a democratic people would be as much endangered as its business and manufactures, if the government ever wholly usurped the place of private companies...A government can no more be competent to keep alive and to renew the circulation of opinions and feelings amongst a great people, than to manage all the speculations of productive industry. No sooner does a government attempt to go beyond its political sphere and to enter upon this new track, than it exercises, even unintentionally, an insupportable tyranny; for a government can only dictate strict rules, the opinions which it favors are rigidly enforced, and it is never easy to discriminate between its advice and its commands. Worse still will be the case if the government really believes itself interested in preventing all circulation of ideas; it will then stand motionless, and oppressed by the heaviness of voluntary torpor..." (Tocqueville)

Questions for Discussion:

1. What blessings flow to societies through the protection of property rights?

2. What are the proper limits of the state, acting as the sovereign representative of the people, in requiring services and taxes of its citizens?

3. Locke commented that "charity gives every man a title to so much out of another's plenty as will keep him from extreme want." What is the proper role of the state in caring for the poor, versus the responsibility of individuals?

IV. Moral Agency — the Freedom of Choice

"Laws provide, as much as possible, that the goods and

health of subjects be not injured by fraud and violence of others; they do not guard them from the negligence or ill-husbandry of the possessors themselves. No man can be forced to be rich or healthful whether he will or no. God himself will not save men against their wills..." (Locke)

"Happiness is the chief end of man, and the saving of his soul is his chief happiness; so that every man is most concerned for his own soul, more than any other can be: And if no obstruction be thrown in his way, he will for the most part do all in his power for his own salvation, and will certainly do it best; and when he has done all he can, he has done all he ought: people cannot be saved by force; nor can all the powers in the world together make one true Christian, or convince one man...The methods of power are repugnant to the nature of conviction, which must either be promoted by exhortation, kindness, example, arguments, or can never be promoted at all..." (Trenchard)

"..neither one person, nor any number of persons, is warranted in saying to another human creature of ripe years, that he shall not do with his life for his own benefit what he chooses to do with it. He is the person most interested in his own well being: the interest which any other person, except in cases of strong personal attachment, can have in it, is trifling, compared with that which he himself has; the interest which society has in him individually (except as to his conduct to others) is fractional, and altogether indirect: while with respect to his own feelings and circumstances, the most ordinary man or women has means of knowledge immeasurably surpassing those that can be possessed by anyone else."(Mill)

"…the sole end for which mankind are warranted, individually or collectively, in interfering with the liberty of action of any of their number, is self-protection. That is the only purpose for which power can be rightfully exercised over any member of a civilized community, against his will, is to prevent harm to others. His own good, either physical or moral, is not a sufficient warrant. He cannot rightfully be compelled to do or forbear because it will be better for him to do so, because it will make him happier, because in the opinion of others, to do so would be wise, or even right. These are good reasons for remonstrating with him, or reasoning with him, or persuading him, or entreating him, but not for compelling him, or visiting him with any evil in case he do otherwise. To justify that, the conduct from which it is desired to deter him must be calculated to produce evil to someone else. The only part of the conduct of any one, for which he is amenable to society, is that which concerns others. In the part which merely concerns himself, his independence is, of right absolute. Over himself, over his body and mind, the individual is sovereign." (Mill)

"..the civil state is based…on the following principles: 1) The freedom of every citizen as a human being, 2) the equality of each member with every other as a subject, 3) the independence of every member of the commonwealth as a citizen…I express the principle of freedom as a human being in this formula: no one can compel me (in accordance with his belief about the welfare of others) to be happy after his fashion; instead, every person may seek happiness in a way that seems best to him, if only he does not violate the freedom of others....I express the principle of equality of subjects in the following formula: every member of the commonwealth has coercive rights in relation to every other member...From this idea of the equality of men as subjects in the commonwealth comes this formula: every member of the commonwealth must be permitted to attain any degree of status to which a subject can aspire, to which his talent, his industry and his luck may bring him; and his fellow subjects may not block his way by appealing to hereditary privileges...Independence of a member of the commonwealth as a citizen; i.e. as co-legislator..here then, craftsman and large (or small) landowners are all equal, each entitled to one vote...here then is an original contract among men on which alone a civil constitution may be based." (Kant)

Questions for Discussion:

1. Why cannot the state compel what it deems to be the best of personal behavior? How does this relate to the concept of personal responsibility?

2. What blessings come from having the ability to choose how we live our lives — both on a personal level, and as a society?

3. What role the state should play in the lives of those with limited capacity, due to illness, age or disability? What about the state's

responsibility to those from "disadvantaged" backgrounds or circumstances – i.e. the unemployed or the working poor?

V. Freedom of Expression
"Freedom of speech is the great bulwark of liberty; they prosper and die together." (Trenchard)

"...the particular evil of silencing the expression of an opinion is, that it is robbing the human race; posterity as well as the existing generation; those who dissent from the opinion still more than those who hold it. If the opinion is right, they are deprived of the opportunity of exchanging error for truth; if wrong, they lose, what is almost as great a benefit, the clearer perception and livelier impression of truth, produced by its collision with error." (Mill)

"Guilt only dreads liberty of speech, which drags it out of its lurking holes, and exposes its deformity and horror to the daylight" (Trenchard)

"Wherever truth is dangerous, liberty is precarious...Honesty and plainness always go together, and the makers and multipliers of mysteries, in the political way, are shrewdly to be suspected of dark designs...some have said, it is not the business of private man to meddle with government. A bold, false and dishonest saying...Public truths ought never to be kept secrets, and they who do it, are guilty of solecism and a contradiction. Every man ought to know what it concerns all to know. Now, nothing upon this earth is

of a more universal nature than government, and every private man has a concern in it, because in it is concerned, nearly and immediately concerned, his virtue, his property and the security of his person...Ill government, subsisting of vice and rapine, are jealous of private virtue and enemies of private property..." (Trenchard)

Questions for Discussion:
1. In what way is freedom of expression "the great bulwark of liberty"? How is our overall liberty impacted when freedom of expression is curtailed?
2. How do we benefit by free communication of all ideas, even in cases when they are in

error?

3. How have we been blessed as individuals and a society through freedom of expression?

V. Justice

"...justice is the offspring of liberty, and her handmaiden; it is the guardian of innocence, and the terror of vice: And when fame, honor, and advantage are rewards of virtue, she will be courted for the dower which she brings; otherwise, like beauty without wealth, she may be praised, but more probably will be calumniated, envied, and very often persecuted; while vie, when it is gainful, like rich deformity and prosperous folly, will be admired and pursued." (Trenchard)

"Justice must be made the principal ground of our actions. For with which support there is the best hope of success to our arms. But without that, any point which may be gained for the moment has no firm ground to rest upon." (Grotius)

Questions for Discussion:
1. What is the relationship between justice and a free society?

End of Chapter Exercises
1. Read the Bill of Rights (Amendments 1-10 of the U.S. Constitution). Make a list of how these enumerated rights have blessed your life.

2. Participate in charitable and community efforts to relieve poverty, lift the burdens of our neighbor, and build up civil society through sharing our plenty and our talents.

Chapter 3: Peace – The Purpose of Government

In a state of nature, man was alone, and insecure. In order to obtain for themselves greater happiness and security, people formed communities and governments wherein they willingly gave up some liberties and freedoms in exchange for security and peace. Societies established by force and without this social compact are usurpations and their leaders are occupiers in a state of war over the people they oppress. Likewise, leaders and governments which overstep the terms of the social compact, taking to themselves powers not given by the people, are illegitimate. The ultimate purpose of government is the security of its citizens.

I. The Social Compact as a Foundation of Liberty

"That the benefit and safety of the people constitutes the supreme law, is an universal and everlasting maxim in government…The sole end of men's entering into political societies, was mutual protection and defense; and whatever power does not contribute to those purposes, is not government, but usurpation." (Trenchard)

"What is government, but a trust committed by all, or the most, to one, or a few, who are to attend upon the affairs of all, that every one may, with the more security, attend upon his own?" (Trenchard)

"How often has the end been sacrificed to the means! Government was instituted for the happiness of society: how often has the happiness of society been offered as a victim to the idol of government! But this is not agreeable to the true order of things: it is not consistent with the orthodox political creed. Let government—let even the constitution be, as they ought to be, the handmaids; let them not be, for they ought not to be, the mistresses of the state." (Wilson)

"Every man being..naturally free, and nothing being able to put him into subjection to any earthly power, but only his own consent...the chief end...of men's uniting into commonwealths, and putting themselves under government, is the preservation of their property. To which in the state of nature there are many things wanting....

...First, there wants an established settled known law...to decide all controversies between them...Secondly, in the state of nature there wants a known and indifferent judge..Thirdly, in the state of nature there often wants power to back and support the sentence when right, and to give it full execution...the inconveniences that they are then exposed to, by the irregular and uncertain exercise of the power every man has of punishing the transgressions of others, make them take sanctuary under the established laws of government, and therein seek the preservation of property." (Locke)

"Since no man has a natural authority over his fellow man, and since force does not give rise to any right, conventions therefore remain the basis of all legitimate authority among men." (Rousseau)

"Liberty if the unalienable right of all mankind. All

governments, under whatsoever forms they are administered, ought to be administered for the good of society; when they are otherwise administered, they cease to be government, and become usurpation. This being the end of all government, even the most despotic have this limitation to their authority. " (Trenchard)

"…instead of destroying natural equality, the fundamental compact, on the contrary, substitutes a moral and legitimate equality to whatever physical inequality nature may have been able to impose upon men, and that, however, unequal in force or intelligence they may be, all men become equal by convention and by right." (Rousseau)

"The final cause, end, or design of men, (who naturally love liberty and dominion over others) is in the introduction of restraint upon themselves, (in which we see them live in commonwealths) is the foresight of their own preservation, and of a more contented life thereby; that is to say of getting themselves out from that miserable condition of war, which is necessarily consequent…to the natural passions of men, when there is no visible power to keep them in awe, and tie them by fear of punishment to the performance of their covenants….without the terror of some power, to cause them to be observed, are contrary to our natural passions that carry us to partiality, pride, revenge and the like. And covenants without the sword, are but words, and of no strength to secure a man at all." (Hobbes)

"Natural independence is exchanged for liberty; the power to harm others is exchanged for their own security; and for their force, which others could overcome, for a right which the social union renders invincible. Their life itself, which they have devoted to the state, is continually protected by it; and when they risk their lives for its defense, what are they doing but returning to the state what they have received from it? What are they doing, that they did not more frequently and with greater danger in the state of nature, when they would inevitably have to fight battles, defending at peril of their lives the means of their preservation? It is true that everyone has to fight, if necessary, for the homeland, but it is also the case that no one ever has to fight on his own behalf." (Rousseau)

"[the social compact] is reducible to the following terms. Each of us places his person and all his power in common under the supreme direction of the general will; and as one we receive each member as an indivisible part of the whole." (Rousseau)

"A state also of equality, wherein all the power and jurisdiction is reciprocal, no one having more than another; there being nothing more evident, than that creatures of the same species and rank, promiscuously born to the same advantage of nature and the use of the same faculties, should also be equal one amongst another without subordination or subjection..." (Locke)

"...were the impulses of conscience clear, uniform, and irresistibly obeyed, man would need no other lawgiver; but that not being the case, he finds it necessary to surrender up a part of his property to furnish means for the protection of the rest; and this he is induced to do by the same prudence which in every other case advises him out of two evils to choose the least. Wherefore, security being the true design and end of government, it unanswerably follows that whatever form thereof appears most likely to ensure it to us, with the least expense and greatest benefit, is preferable to all others...Here then is the origin and rise of government; namely, a mode rendered necessary by the inability of moral virtue to govern the world; here too is the design and end of government, viz., freedom and security..." (Paine)

Questions for Discussion:
1. What would be the state of man in nature in terms of their safety, security and property rights?
2. What is the state of man when living in a government not formed through social compact (i.e. dictatorship, authoritarian regime)?
3. What are the benefits of living under a government formed through agreement of its citizens?

II. Authority of Law in The Social Compact

"There is but one law that by its nature requires unanimous consent. This is the social compact. For civil association is the most voluntary act in the world. Since every man is born free and master of himself, no one can, under any pretext whatever, place another under subjection without his consent. To decide that the son of a slave is born a slave is to decide he was not a man. If, therefore, at the time of the social compact, there are opponents to it, their opposition does not invalidate the contract, it merely prevents them from being included in it. They are foreigners among citizens. Once a state is instituted, residency implies consent. To inhabit the territory is to submit to sovereignty...the citizen consents to all the laws, even to those that pass in spite of his opposition, and even to those that punish him when he dares violate any of them. The constant will of all the members of the state is the general will; through it they are citizens and free. When a law is proposed in the people's assembly, what he asked of them is not precisely whether they approve or reject, but whether or not it conforms to the general will that is theirs. Each man, in giving his vote, states his opinion if this matter and the declaration of the general will is drawn from the counting of votes." (Rousseau)

"...there is only political society where every one of the members hath quitted this natural power, resigned it up into the hands of the community in all cases that exclude him not from appealing for protection to the law established by it. And thus all private judgment of every particular member being excluded, the community comes to be the umpire, by settled standing rules, indifferent, and the same to all parties; and by men having authority from the community, for the execution of those rules, decides all the differences that may happen between any members of that society

concerning any matter of right; and punishes those offenses which any member hath committed against the society, with such penalties as the law has established: whereby it is easy to discern, who are and who are not in political society together." (Locke)

"The only way to erect such a common power as may be able to defend them from the inaction of foreigners, and the injuries of one another and thereby secure them in such sort, and by their own industry, and by the fruits of the earth, they may nourish themselves and live contentedly; is to confer all their power and strength upon one man, or assembly of men that they may reduce all their wills, by plurality of voices unto one will…in those things which concern the common peace and safety and therein submit their wills, every one to his will, and their judgments to his judgment…as if every man should say to every man, I authorize and give up my right of governing myself to this man or this assembly of men, on this condition, that thou give up they rights to him and authorize all his actions in like matter. This done, the multitude so united is called a commonwealth." (Hobbes)

"Political power, then, I take to be a right of making laws with penalties of death, and consequently all less penalties, for the regulating and preserving of property, and of employing the force of the community, in the execution of such laws and in defense of the commonwealth from foreign injury; and all this only for the public good." (Locke)

"And thus the commonwealth comes by a power to set down what punishment shall belong to the several transgressions which they think worthy of it, committed amongst the members of that society, (which is the power of making laws) as well as it has the power to punish any injury done unto any of its members, by any one that is not of it, (which is the power of making war and peace) and all this for the preservation of the property of all the members of that society, as far as is possible." (Locke)

"Seek first the kingdom of pure practical reason, and your end (the blessing of perpetual peace) will come to you of itself." For this characteristic is inherent in mortals — especially as regards to its fundamental principles of public right — that the less it makes conduct depend on the proposed end, be it a physical or moral advantage, the more conduct will in general harmonize with morality...This proposition means only that adherence to political maxims must not be based on the benefit or the happiness that each nation makes an object (of its desire) and its supreme (though empirical) principle of political wisdom; instead, adherence must derive from the pure concept of the duty of right, let physical consequences be what they may." (Kant)

Questions for Discussion:

1. What benefits come to citizens as they subject themselves to the law of the state?
2. Why does Kant believe it is important that law and policy of the state be guided by fundamental values, rather than focused purely on the results sought?

III. Limited Government and the Protection of Property

"..the general will can direct the forces of the state according to the purpose for which it was instituted, which is the common good." (Rousseau)

"…though men, when they enter into society, give up the equality, liberty, and executive power they had in the state of nature, into the hands of society, to be so far disposed of the by the legislative, as the good of the society shall require; yet it being only with an intention in every one the better to preserve himself, his liberty and property (for no rational creature can be supposed to change the condition with an intention to be worse) the power of the society, or legislative constituted by them, can never be supposed to extend farther, than the common good; but is obliged to secure every one's property, by providing against those...defects...that made the state of nature so unsafe and so uneasy." (Locke)

"...What man loses through the social contract is his natural liberty and an unlimited right to everything that tempts him and that he can acquire. What he gains is civil liberty and proprietary ownership of all he possesses. So as not to be in error in these compensations, it is necessary to draw careful distinction between natural liberty (which is limited solely by the force of the individual involved), and civil liberty (which is limited by the general will), and between possession (which is merely the effort of the force of right of the first occupant), and proprietary ownership (which is based solely on positive title)." (Rousseau)

"..each person alienates, by the social compact, only that portion of his power, his goods, and liberty whose use is of consequence to the community; but we must also grant that only the sovereign is the judge of what is of consequence. A citizen should render to the state all the services he can as the sovereign demands them. However, for its part, the sovereign cannot impose on the subjects any fetters that are of no use to the community." (Rousseau)

"If we suffer tamely a lawless attack upon our property and fortunes we encourage it, and involve others in our doom...When men begin to be wicked, we cannot tell where that wickedness will end; we have reason to fear the worst, and provide against it." (Trenchard)

"I am aware that many of my countrymen are not in the least embarrassed by this difficulty [of expanding government]. They contend that the more enfeebled and incompetent the citizens become, the more able and active the government ought to be rendered, in order that society at large may execute what individuals can no longer accomplish. They believe this answers the whole difficulty, but I think they are mistaken. A government might perform the part of some of the largest American companies; and several States, members of the Union, have already attempted it; but what political power could ever carry on the vast multitude of lesser undertakings which the American citizens perform every day, with the assistance of the principle of association?" (Tocqueville)

Question for Discussion:
1. What is the role of the state in protecting private property?
2. What services do we expect our government to provide, versus civil society.

End of Chapter Exercise
1. Participate in activities that strengthen our commitment to participatory government. Ideas may include participation in election and issues campaign, writing Op Eds, letters to legislators of key issues, attending town meetings etc.

Chapter 4: Leadership in Government

In free societies leaders are to be sought with qualities of virtue, courage, integrity, wisdom, experience, patience, etc — creating a sort of democratic aristocracy, not because of power, wealth or influence, but because of the excellence of character. There will always be those who lack excellence in character, but are supported by faction and grasp for power. To avoid being taken in by populist feelings, manipulated by propaganda, and captured by factional movements, we must know well before the moment of decision exactly what qualities and characteristics we value in our leaders; establishing a yard-stick by which all who seek office can be measured. Further, as we understand those characteristics of excellence we seek, we can more effectively develop those virtues in our own lives and in the rising generation, thus increasing the pool of qualified leaders.

I. Virtuous Leaders

"...the shepherds skill is devoted solely to the welfare of the flock which he is charge, and so long as it succeeds in discharging its function, its own welfare is adequately provided for." (Plato)

"It is his subject and his subject's proper interests to which he looks in all he says and does." (Plato)

"...it belongs to the idea of a king that there is one person who rules, and that he is a shepherd who seeks the common good of the people and not his individual good." (Aquinas)

"The good, then, is the end of all endeavor, the object which every heart is set, whose existence it divines, though it finds it difficult to grasp just what it is…" (Plato)

"A beneficent prince, as Plutarch said with all his learning, is a kind of living likeness of God, who is at once good and powerful. His goodness makes him want to help all, his power makes him able to do so….When you who are a prince, a Christian prince, hear and read that you are the likeness of God and his vicar, do not swell with pride on this account, but rather let the fact make you all the more concerned to live up to that wonderful archetype of yours; and remembering that though following him is hard, not following him is a sin." (Erasmus)

"The prince should not be ashamed to obey what is good and right, for God himself obeys it; nor should he think himself any less a prince if he makes every effort to approach the image of the highest prince of all." (Erasmus)

"…good men will not consent to govern for cash or honors. They do not want to be called mercenary for extracting cash payment for the work of the government, or thieves for making money on the side; and they will not work for honors, for they are not ambitious." (Plato)

"And so the best institution of rulers belongs to a city or kingdom in which one person is chosen by reason of his virtue to rule over all, and other persons govern under him by reason of their virtue. And yet such a regime belongs to all citizens, because its rulers are chosen from the citizens, and because all citizens choose its rulers. For this is the best constitution, a happy mixture of kingdom, since one person rules; and of aristocracy, since many govern by reason of their virtue; and of democracy (i.e., government by the people), since rulers can be chosen from the people since the choice of rulers belongs to the people." (Plato)

"...the divine law established such a regime. For Moses and his successors governed the people, individually ruling over all as it were and this regime is a form of kingdom. And seventy-two elders were chosen by reason of their virtue...and this was aristocratic. And the regime was democratic in that the rulers were chosen from all the people..."take wise men from among you,"..." (Aquinas)

"Remember your ancestors — and govern our country in such a way that your fellow-citizens will rejoice that you were born." (Cicero)

"...a truly great man is ever the same under all circumstances; and if his fortune caries, exalting him at one moment and oppressing him at another, he himself never varies, but always preserves a firm courage, which is so closely interwoven with his character that everyone can readily see that the fickleness of fortune has no power over him..." (Machiavelli)

"Conduct your own rule as if you were striving to ensure that no successor could be your equal, but all the time prepare your children for their future reign as if to ensure that a better man would indeed succeed you." (Erasmus)

"However many statues he may set up and however much he may toil over the construction he erects the prince can leave no finer monument to his good qualities than a son who is in every way of the same stock and who recreates his father's excellence in his own excellent actions. He does not die who leaves a living likeness of himself." (Erasmus)

"The next lesson is to love the country he rules and to have the same attitude towards it that a good farmer has towards the land he has inherited or that a good man has towards his family, and to be especially concerned that he will hand over to whoever comes next as improvement on what he himself received." (Erasmus)

"The nature of the prince is recognized more surely from what he says that from what he wears: anything caught from the prince's lips is spread abroad. He must continually take the greatest care that what he says savors of integrity and gives evidence of thinking that is worthy of a good prince." (Erasmus)

"...let this be the only way he assesses his people's happiness: not whether he keeps them in great wealth or in optimal health, but by their honest and moderation; by the absence of greed, aggressiveness, contentions and by the presence of the fullest possible harmony." (Erasmus)

"The good, wise and upright prince is simply a sort of embodiment of the law." (Erasmus)

"Even if he is at home or in retreat the prince should imitate the worthy Scopio, who used to say that he was never less alone than when he was on his own and never less idle than when he had time to spare, for whenever he was free of public business, he would always be pondering some idea concerning the security or dignity of the state." (Erasmus)

"The conduct of General Epaminondas has been praised by learned men; when he was appointed, through envy, to a lowly office, one held in public contempt, he carried out its duties so well that it was regarded afterwards as one of the most honorable of positions and the greatest men vied for it; thus he showed that it is not the office that bring honor to the man, but man to the office." (Erasmus)

Questions for Discussion:
1. Why is the character of our leaders important to the individual pursuit of happiness?
2. What characteristics should we look for in our elected officials?
3. What benefits come from our ability to select qualified representatives?

II. Leadership Challenges

"A leader who does not restrain himself cannot restrain

his army; if his own conduct will not bear exacting criticism, he is in no position to censure others." (Cicero)

"The best fortress to be found is the love of the people, for although you may have fortresses they will not save you if you are hated by the people." (Machiavelli)

[Courage] "...consists of detecting, squarely facing, and conquering the deceit of the evil principle in ourselves, which is the dangerously devious and treacherous because it excuses all our transgressions with an appeal to human nature's frailty" (Kant)

"In a popular state, one spring more is necessary, namely virtue....when virtue is banished, ambition invades the minds of those who are disposed to receive it, and avarice possesses the whole community..." (Montesquieu)

"The principle of democracy is corrupted not only when the spirit of equality is extinct, but likewise when they fall into a spirit of extreme equality, and when each citizen would fain be upon a level with those whom he has chosen to command him. Then the people, incapable of bearing the very power they have delegated, want to manage everything themselves, to debate for the senate, to execute for the magistrate, and to decide for the judges." (Montesquieu)

Questions for Discussion:

1. Is there anything we can do to help prevent leaders from being corrupted by power and avarice?

2. How do we properly draw the boundary between being active citizens, engaged in the debate of our times, and our need to respect our elected officials and honor their decisions?

III. Mode of Governing

"A prince, therefore, must not mind incurring the charge of cruelty for the purpose of keeping his subjects united and faithful; for, with a very few examples, he will be more merciful than those who, from excess of tenderness, allow disorders to arise, from whence spring bloodshed and rapine, for these as a rule injure the whole community, while the executions carried out by the prince injure only individuals." (Machiavelli)

"Thus the dominant will of the prince is not and should not be anything other than the general will or the law. His force is merely the public force concentrated in him. As soon as he wants to derive from himself some absolute and independent act, the bond that links everything together begins to come loose. If it should finally happen that the prince had a private will more active than that of the sovereign, and that he made use of some public force that is available to him in order to obey this private will, so that there would be, so to speak, two sovereigns — one de jure and the other de facto, at that moment the social union would vanish and the body politic would be dissolved." (Rousseau)

"The persons entrusted and representing shall either never have any interest detached from the person entrusted or represented, or never the means to pursue it. Now to compass this great point effectually, no other way is left, but these two: or rather, namely, to make the deputies so numerous, that there may be no possibility of corrupting the majority, or, by changing them so often, that there is no sufficient time to corrupt them and to carry out the ends of that corruption." (Trenchard)

"This was the ancient constitution of England...the same Parliament seldom met twice, for the serving in it being an office of burden, and not of profit, it was thought reasonable that all men qualified should, in their turns, leave their families and domestic concerns, to serve the public and their boroughs bore their charges..." (Trenchard)

[Unity] "The state should, I think, be allowed to grow so long as growth is compatible with unity, but no further." (Plato)

Questions for Discussion:
1. What steps can we take to ensure that our elected and appointed officials are unable to use their positions for personal gain?
2. How important is it that our elected representatives change office frequently? What are the advantages and disadvantages of long tenure or short tenure for our elected officials?

End of Chapter Exercises
1. Regarding your elected officials, make a list of characteristics you feel are essential, and another list of those you feel are important. Consider the impact this list should have on your choice of candidates at election times.

Chapter 5: Constitutional Government

Our founding fathers recognized the blessing of government, but of limited government. They established a government in which the separation of powers between the executive, legislative and judicial branches, federal authorities and state police power, protected individual freedom, choice, and made the likelihood of tyranny most remote. It was to be a government of law and not men. While such a government is neither efficient nor swift, its protections have ensured an unprecedented spirit of innovation, development, and liberty.

I. Rule of Law

"Where the law is not sovereign, there is no constitution." (Aristotle)

"...wherever law ends, tyranny begins..." (Locke)

"Rightly constituted laws should be the final sovereign, but rulers, whether one or many, should be sovereign in those matters on which law is unable, owing to the difficulty of framing general rules for all contingencies, to make an exact pronouncement...laws which are in accordance with right constitutions {i.e. for the benefit of the whole} must necessarily be just, and laws which are in accordance with perverted constitutions must be unjust...in political matters the end in view is the greatest good and the good which is most to be pursued..." (Aristotle)

"The civic body is everywhere sovereign...in fact the

civic body is the constitution itself. In democratic cities, the people are sovereign, in oligarchies, the few have that position." (Aristotle)

"It may perhaps be urged that it is a poor sort of policy to vest sovereignty in a human being, rather than in law; for human beings are subject to the passions that beset their souls.." (Aristotle)

"The good life is the chief end, both for the community as a whole and for each of us individual" (Aristotle)

"He who command that law should rule may thus be regarded that commanding that God and reason alone should rule; he who commands that man should rule adds the character of the beast...To seek for justice is to seek for a neutral standard; and law is a neutral standard." (Aristotle)

"Since the mass of the people are thus included among those who have a share in the business of government, it follows that sovereignty, under this form, will be vested in the law, rather than in mere human beings. A moderate oligarchy of this type is totally different from the personal rule of a monarch; and as its members have neither so much property that they are able to enjoy a leisure free time from all business cares, nor so little that they depend on the city for support, they will be bound to ask that the law should rule for them, and they will not claim to rule for themselves." (Aristotle)

"When the deputies thus act for their own interest, by

acting for the interest of their principals, when they can make no law but what they themselves, and their posterity, must be subject to; when they can give no money, but what they must pay their share of; when they can do no mischief, but what must fall upon their own heads in common with their countrymen; their principals may then expect good laws, little mischief, and much frugality." (Trenchard)

Questions for Discussion:

1. What does Locke mean when he says "...wherever law ends, tyranny begins...?" How is law a "...neutral standard...?"
2. What is the value of law in our society? How does that impact our decisions in choosing our legislators?

II. The Merits of Democracy

"It will be said, perhaps, that democracy is neither wise nor equitable, but that the holders of property are also the best fitted to rule. I say, on the contrary, first, that the word demos, or people, includes the whole state, oligarchy only a part; next, that if the best guardians of property are the rich, and the best counselors the wise, none can hear and decide so well as the many; and that all these talents, severally and collectively, have their just place in a democracy" (Thucydides)

"...each of them by himself may not be of a good quality, but when they all come together it is possible that they may surpass — collectively and as a body, although not individually — the quality of the few best.." (Aristotle)

"Let people alone, and they will take care of themselves, and do it best; and if they do not, a sufficient punishment will follow their neglect, without the magistrates interposition and penalties." (Trenchard)

Questions for Discussion:
1. What benefits to decision making are derived from the democratic process?

III. Legal Protection of Property Rights

"...the increase of lands, and the right of employing them, is the great art of government: and that prince, who shall be so wise and godlike, as by established laws of liberty to secure protection and encouragement to the honest industry of mankind, against the oppression of power and narrowness of party, will quickly be too hard for his neighbors..." (Locke)

"...where the middle class is large, there is less likelihood of faction and dissension than in any other constitution." (Aristotle)

Questions for Discussion:
1. How do legal protections of property inspire industry in a society?

IV. The Importance of Check and Balances on Power
"...governance of the kingdom should be so arranged that there is no opportunity for a king in power to become a tyrant. At the same time that a King is installed, his power should be so moderated that he cannot easily lapse into tyranny." (Machiavelli)

"Liberty is a right of doing whatever the laws permit...to prevent abuse, it is necessary from the very nature of things that power should be a check on power. A government may be so constituted, as no man shall be compelled to do things which the law does not oblige him, nor forced to abstain from things which the law permits." (Montesquieu)

"Republicanism is that political principle whereby the executive power (the government) is separated from legislative power." (Kant)

"The Tarentines have also divided all offices into two classes — one with appointments made by election, and the other with appointments made by lot — with the intention that the latter will give the people a share in office, while the former will help ensure a better administration." (Plato)

"In every government there are three sorts of power, the legislative...the judiciary power...and...the executive power of the state..The political liberty of the subjects is a tranquility of mind arising from the opinion each person has of his safety. In order to have this liberty, it is requisite that the government be so constituted as one man need not be afraid of another. When the legislative and executive powers are united in the same person or in the same body of magistrate, there can be no liberty; because apprehensions may arise, lest the same monarch or senate should erect tyrannical laws, to execute them in a tyrannical manner. Again, there is no liberty if the judiciary power be not separated from the legislative and executive...Where is joined to the executive power, the judge might behave with violence and oppression." (Montesquieu)

[On limits of executive/legislative power] "...First...it is limited to the public good of the society. It is a power that hath no other end but preservation and therefore can never have a right to destroy, enslave, or designedly to impoverish the subjects…Secondly…[it cannot] rule by extemporary arbitrary decrees, but is bound to dispense justice, and decide the right of the subjects by promulgated standing laws, and known authorized judges…Thirdly, the supreme power cannot take from any man any part of his property without his own consent…It is true, governments cannot be supported without great charge, and it is fit everyone who enjoys his share of the protection, should pay out of his estate the proportion for the maintenance of it. But still it must be with his own consent…i.e. the consent of the majority, giving it either by themselves or their representatives chose by the, for if any one shall claim power to lay and levy taxes in the people, by his own authority, and without consent of the people, he thereby invades the fundamental law of property, and subverts the end of government…Fourthly, the legislative cannot transfer the power of making laws to any other hands…nor can the people be bound by any laws, but such as are enacted by those whom they have chosen. ..." (Locke)

"The executive as well as the legislative power ought to be restrained. But there is a remarkable contrast between the proper modes of restraining them. The legislature, in order to be restrained, must be divided. The executive power, in order to be restrained, should be one. Unity in this department is at once a proof and an ingredient of safety and of energy in the operations of government. The restraints on the legislative authority must, from its nature, be chiefly internal; that is, they must proceed from some part or division of itself. But the restraints on the executive power are external...

The third great division of the powers of government is the judicial authority... The judicial authority consists in applying, according to the principles of right and justice, the constitution and laws to facts and transactions in cases, in which the manner or principles of this application are disputed by the parties interested in them...

Let us suppose the legislative and executive powers united in the same person: can liberty or security be expected? No. In the character of executive magistrate, he receives all the power, which, in the character of legislator, he thinks proper to give. May he not, then — and, if he may, will he not then — such is the undefined and undefinable charm of power — enact tyrannical laws to furnish himself with an opportunity of executing them in a tyrannical manner? Liberty and security in government depend not on the limits, which the rulers may please to assign to the exercise of their own powers, but on the boundaries, within which their powers are circumscribed by the constitution...Let us suppose the legislative and judicial powers united: what would be the consequence? The lives, liberties, and properties of the citizens would be committed to arbitrary judges, whose decisions would, in effect, be dictated by their own private opinions, and would not be governed by any fixed or known principles of law...

Let us suppose a union of the executive and judicial powers: this union might soon be an overbalance for the legislative authority; or, if that expression is too strong, it might certainly prevent or destroy the proper and legitimate influences of that authority. The laws might be eluded or perverted; and the execution of them might become, in the hands of the magistrate or his minions, an engine of tyranny and injustice. Where and how is redress to be obtained? From the legislature? They make new laws to correct the mischief: but these new laws are to be executed by the same persons, and will be executed in the same manner as the former. Will redress be found in the courts of justice? In those courts, the very persons who were guilty of the oppression in their administration, sit as judges, to give a sanction to that oppression by their decrees. Nothing is more to be dreaded than maxims of law and reasons of state blended together by judicial authority. Among all the terrible instruments of arbitrary power, decisions of courts, whetted and guided and impelled by considerations of policy, cut with the keenest edge, and inflict the deepest and most deadly wounds...Let us suppose, in the last place, all the three powers of government to be united in the same man or body of men: miserable indeed would this case be!" (Wilson)

Questions for Discussion:

1. What benefits do we derive from the checks and balances on government power?
2. If government power is limited by design, how should that impact our expectation on government efficiency? For example, under the US Constitution, it is easy for the President to marshal military forces to

protect the nation, but it should be more difficult to launch a war. What do we lose in efficiency in a process which requires consultation with Congress? Why are such limits important?

V. On Representatives

"The regulating of the conditions of a society belongs to no one but those who are in association one with another...The general will is always right, but the judgment that guides it is not always enlightened...Everyone is equally in need of guides...whence arises the necessity of having a legislator." (Rousseau)

"The legislator is in every respect an extraordinary man of the state. If he ought to be so by his genius, he is no less so by his office, which is neither magistracy nor sovereignty. This office, which constitutes the republic, does not enter into its constitution. It is a particular and superior function having nothing in common with the dominion over men. For he who has command over the laws must no longer have any authority over men. Otherwise, his laws...would often serve to perpetuate injustices, and he could never avoid private opinions altering the sanctity of his work." (Rousseau)

"...in popular governments all the citizens are born magistrates; however, this type of government limits them to a small number, and they become magistrates only through election a means which probity, enlightenment, experience, and all the other reasons for public preference and esteem are so many new guarantees of being well governed." (Rousseau)

"It is also certain that the execution of the public business becomes slower in proportion as more people are charged with the responsibility for it; that in attaching too much impotence to prudence, too little importance is attached to fortune, opportunities are missed, and the fruits of deliberation are often lost by dint of deliberation." (Rousseau)

Questions for Discussion:
>   1. What are the benefits of representative government?

End of Chapter Exercise
>   1. Visit, watch or listen to a congressional debate, committee hearing, or Supreme

Court argument. Afterwards, write a journal entry on your feelings regarding our democratic process, representative government, and separation of powers.

Chapter 6: The Natural Law and the Laws of Man

The foundation of free societies is recognition that all men are created equal. In a state of nature, men had all liberty, yet were granted a gift of understanding right from wrong — deemed by philosophers the natural law. This natural law was supplement at times by clearer direction through revelation of divine law. Men formed agreements, and eventually societies, through covenant, adding laws of man to those of the natural and divine law. The laws of man are necessary protections due to the imperfections and potential corruption of individuals. In contemplating the values of freedom, an appreciation of man, as a creature that (barring some defect) is innately capable of comprehending good and evil, helps us to appreciate the potential for good in society as individuals learn to tame passions and hearken to that voice of conscience within them. It is ultimately individual choice and action that drive innovation, goodness, charity, and benevolence in society.

I. Man in a State of Nature

"Men living together according to reason, without a common superior on earth, with authority to judge between them, is properly the state of nature." (Locke)

"...wherever any two men are, who have no standing rule betwixt them, there they are still in the state of nature..." (Locke)

[The first law between men in a state of nature is] "...that men perform their covenants made; without which covenants are in vain, and but empty works; and the right of all men to all things remaining, we are still in a condition of warfare...the definition of injustice is, none other than the non performance of covenant." (Hobbes)

"Though as I have said...all men by nature are equal, I cannot be supposed to understand all sorts of equality: age or virtue may give men a just presidency: excellency of parts and merit may place others above the common level: birth may subject some, and alliance or benefit others, to pay an observance to those to whom nature, gratitude or other respects, may have made it duel and yet all this consists with the equality, which all men are in, in respect of jurisdiction or dominion one over another; which was the equality I there spoke of, as proper to the business at hand, being that equal right that every man hath, to his natural freedom, without being subjected to the will and authority if any other man." (Locke)

Questions for Discussion:

1. For generations of time, men have been born into societies with preexisting laws and mores. Why was it that philosophers spent time discussing what man was like in a state of nature, before the organization of society? How does contemplation of man in such a state help us to further appreciate the development of law, and the social compacts of societies that are later formed?

2. Locke acknowledges the inequality of men in terms of talent. Why is it important that men

are equal in freedom even though they are not equal in skill?

II. The Natural Law

"But though this be a state of liberty, yet it is not a state of license; though man in that state have an uncontrollable liberty to dispose of his person or possessions, yet he has not liberty to destroy himself, or so much as any creature in his possession...no one ought to harm another in his life, health, liberty or possessions: for men being all the workmanship of one omnipotent, and infinitely wise maker; all the servants of one sovereign master...they are his property...being furnished with like faculties, sharing all in one community of nature, there cannot be supposed any such subordination among us that may authorize us to destroy one another...bound to preserve himself...when his own preservation comes not in competition, ought he, as much as he can, to preserve the rest of mankind, and may not, unless it be to do justice on an offender, take away, or impair the life, or what tends to the preservation of the life, the liberty, health limb or goods of another." (Locke)

"The **natural law** is promulgate by God when he implants it the minds of human beings so that they know it by nature." (Aquinas)

[Natural Law--Nature] "...who has given us this law, which is not written, but innate, which we have not received by instruction, hearing or reading, but the elements of it have been engraven in our hearts and minds with her own hand: a law which is not the effect of habit and acquirement, but forms a part in the original complexion of our frame." (Grotius)

"Do all know the eternal law?....I answer that we can know things in two ways: in one way in themselves; in a second way in their effects, which are like the things. For example, those who are not looking at the sun know it in the effects of its rays. Therefore, we should say no one except the blessed, who see God by his essence, can know the eternal law as it is in itself. But every rational creature knows it in some of its radiating effects, whether greater or lesser effects. For every knowledge of truth is radiation and participation of eternal law, which is incommunicable truth..." (Aquinas)

"...there belong to the natural law, indeed primarily, very general precepts, precepts that everyone knows, and more particular, secondary precepts, which are like proximate conclusions from the first principles. Therefore regarding the general principles, the natural law in general can in no way be excised from the hearts of human beings. But the natural law is wiped out regarding particular actions insofar as desires or other emotions prevent reason from applying the general principles to particular actions.." (Aquinas)

"examine [things] by those rules which you have; and first and chiefly, by this: whether it concerns the things which are within your own power, or those which are not; and if it concerns anything beyond our power, be prepared to say that it is nothing to you." (Epictetus)

"The power of moral perception is, indeed, a most important part of our constitution...By that power, we have conceptions of merit and demerit, of duty and moral obligation. By that power, we perceive some things in human conduct to be right, and others to be wrong...When an action is represented to us, flowing from love, humanity, gratitude, an ultimate desire of the good of others; though it happened in a country far distant, or in an age long past, we admire the lovely exhibition, and praise its author. The contrary conduct, when represented to us, raises our abhorrence and aversion..." (Wilson)

"This moral sense, from its very nature, is intended to regulate and control all our other powers. It governs our passions as well as our actions. Other principles may solicit and allure; but the conscience assumes authority, it must be obeyed. Of this dignity and commanding nature we are immediately conscious, as we are of the power itself...In short; if we had not the faculty of perceiving certain things in conduct to be right, and others to be wrong; and of perceiving our obligation to do what is right, and not to do what is wrong; we should not be moral and accountable beings." (Wilson)

Questions for Discussion:
>   1. According to Grotius and other early philosophers, God hath "engraven in our hearts and minds" the natural law by which all men can distinguish between good and

evil. This basic knowledge of right and wrong "is not written, but innate." Though natural law theory has become an unpopular concept in a world of moral relativism, why is such an understanding of human nature important to us as individuals, families, and societies?

Divine Law

[First] "Divine law was necessary to give direction to human life...but because human beings are ordered to the end of eternal blessedness, which surpasses their

proportional natural human capacity...God needed to lay down law superior to the natural law and human laws to direct human beings toward their end...Second because of the uncertainty of human judgment..in order that human beings can know beyond any doubt what they should do or not do...Third, human beings can make laws regarding what they are able judge. But human beings can judge between perceptible external acts, not hidden internal movements. And yet human beings need to live righteously regarding both kinds of act in order to attain complete virtue. And so human laws could not prohibit or adequately order internal acts, and divine law needed to supplement human laws. Fourth, human laws cannot punish or prohibit all evil deeds." (Aquinas)

Questions for Discussion:

1. If men are born with an innate knowledge of right and wrong, why has it been necessary that divine law be revealed?

Laws of Man

"...every law supposes some evil, and can only punish or restrain the evils which already exist...Law is therefore a sign of the corruption of man, and many laws are the signs of the corruption of a state...The essence of right and wrong does not depend upon the words and clauses inserted in a code or a statute-book, much less upon the conclusions and explications of lawyers, but upon reason and the nature of things, antecedent to all laws." (Trenchard)

"Isidore says in his Etymologies: "Laws were established so that fear of them curb human audacity, and that innocence be safe in the midst of the wicked, and that the fear of punishment [deter] the wicked [from] inflict[ing] harm." (Aquinas)

[Human] "...law can be wanting because emotions or evil habituation, or evil disposition has perverted the reason of some. For example, the Germans of old did not consider robbery wicked, as Ceaser's Gallic Wars relates, although robbery is expressly contrary to the natural law." (Aquinas)

"In a state of natural liberty, everyone is allowed to act according to his own inclination, provided he transgress not those limits, which are assigned to him by the law of nature: in a state of civil liberty, he is allowed to act according to his inclination, provided he transgress not those limits, which are assigned to him by the municipal law. True it is, that, by the municipal law, some things may be prohibited, which are not prohibited by the law of nature: but equally true it is, that, under a government which is wise and good, every citizen will gain more liberty than he can lose by these prohibitions. He will gain more by the limitation of other men's freedom, than he can lose by the diminution of his own. He will gain more by the enlarged and undisturbed exercise of his natural liberty in innumerable instances, than he can lose by the restriction of it in a few. Upon the whole, therefore, man's natural liberty, instead of being abridged, may be increased and secured in a government, which is good and wise. As it is with regard to his natural

liberty, so it is with regard to his other natural rights."
(Wilson)

Questions for Discussion:
1. We have previously examined the blessing of the rule of law. How then is law "...a sign of the corruption of man...?" If all men were perfectly just, would there be a necessity for human law?

End of Chapter Exercise
1. What is termed natural law may be thought of as conscience. Contemplate your own innate ability to know right from wrong. How have you felt when you have made choices you have known to be wrong, but which have satisfied your immediate desires? What do you feel when you have made what you have known to be a right choice, even when it has not been in your immediate interest? Contemplate these evidences of natural law and write in your journal an entry regarding the blessings of being able to discern between good and evil.

Chapter 7: On Warfare

A primary purpose for the formation of a political union is to provide for the common defense. Yet, throughout history, armies have been misused to aggrandize states and their leaders, accumulate wealth and property, or to settle personal disagreements between monarchs. In a free society, such misuses should be rare indeed. To ensure military forces are properly outfitted and employed, citizens must maintain awareness of significant national security debates. Additionally, they are better citizens when they have an understanding of the blessings that flow from peace, the direct and second/third order costs of war, the justness of the causes where military force may be employed, and a commitment to our nation's armed forces. A citizenry so informed is a great bulwark against adventurism and error that lead to or prolong a conflict.

I. Democracies and their Tendencies Toward Peace

"If the consent of the citizenry is required in order to determine whether or not there will be war, it is natural that they consider all its calamities before committing themselves to so risky a game. Among these are doing the fighting themselves, paying the costs of the war from their own resources having to repair at great sacrifice the war's devastation, and, finally, the ultimate evil that would make peace itself better, never being able — because of new and constant wars — to expunge the burden of debt." (Kant)

"The spirit of trade cannot coexist with war, and sooner or later this spirit dominates every people. For among all those powers (or means) that belong to a nation, financial power may be the most reliable in forcing nations to pursue the noble cause of peace (though not from moral motives) and whenever in the world war threatens to break out, others will try to head it off through mediation, just as if they were permanently leagued for this purpose." (Kant)

"The law of nations is naturally founded on this principle, that the different nations ought in time of peace to do one another all the good they can, and in time of war do as little injury as possible, without prejudicing their interests." (Montesquieu)

"The whole [Spartan] system of legislation is directed to fostering only one part of goodness, goodness in war, because that sort of goodness is useful for gaining power. As a result the Spartans remained secure as long as they were at war; but they collapsed as soon as they acquired an empire. They did not know how to use their leisure and they had never accustomed themselves to any discipline other than and superior to that of war." (Aristotle)

Questions for Discussion:
1. The US constitution provided authority to the Congress to declare war and to raise and provide for the armed forces. Congressional support for defense requirements is carried out through committee hearings, debate and the legislative process. Why are such processes vital to ensuring the peace?

2. How do we prevent our nation from becoming overly militaristic?

II. Dissent and Revolution

"...shaking off a power, which force, and not right, hath set over any one, though it hath the name of rebellion, yet is no offense before God, but is that which he allows and countenances, though even promises and covenants" (Locke)

"..a magistrate...acting without authority may be opposed..." (Locke)

"...yet the legislative being only a fiduciary power to act for certain ends, there remains still in the people a supreme power to remove or alter the legislative when they find the legislative act contrary to the trust reposed to them for all power given with trust for the attaining an end, being limited to that end, whenever that end is manifestly neglected, or opposed, the trust must necessarily be forfeited, and the powers devolve into the hands of those that gave it, who may place it anew where they shall think best for their safety and security." (Locke)

"It must be considered that there is nothing more difficult to carry out, nor more doubtful of success, nor more dangerous to handle, than to initiate a new order of things. For the reformer has enemies in all those who profit by the old order, and only lukewarm defenders in all those who would profit by the new order, this lukewarmness arising partly from fear of their adversaries who have the laws in their favor; and partly from the incredulity of mankind, who do not truly believe in anything new until they have had actual experience of it." (Machiavelli)

Questions for Discussion:
1. In a democratic system, how do we properly hold government officials accountable for their actions?
2. The US was founded by revolution. As a nation we often debate assisting similar struggles throughout the world. As Machiavelli points out, such changes are not brought about without much difficulty. As outside observers, what is the proper role of the US in supporting causes of liberty abroad?

III. Evils of War

"I would merely exhort the princes who bear the name of Christian to set aside all trumped-up claims and spurious pretexts and apply themselves seriously and whole heartedly to making an end of this long-standing and terrible mania among Christians for war, and to establish peace and harmony among those who are united by so many common interests." (Erasmus)

"...in the nature of man, we find three principal causes of quarrel. First, Competition; Secondly, Diffidence; Thirdly, Glory. The first maketh men invade for gain; the second for safety, the third for reputation...Hereby

it is manifest, that during the time men live without a common Power to keep them all in awe, they are in that condition which is called war, and such a war as is of every man against every man...In such a condition, there is no place for Industry, because the fruit thereof is uncertain... The passions that encline men to peace are fear of death, desire of such things as are necessary to commodious living; and a hope by their industry to obtain them." (Hobbes)

"If a city which from its origin has enjoyed liberty but has of itself become corrupt, has great difficulties in devising good laws for the maintenance of liberty, it is not to be wondered at if a city that had its origin in servitude finds it, not only difficult, but actually impossible, ever to organize a government that will secure its liberty and tranquility." (Machiavelli)

"He should then consider how desirable, how honorable, how wholesome a thing is peace; on the other hand, how calamitous as well as wicked a thing is war, and how even the most just of wars brings with it a train of evils — if indeed any war can really be called just. Finally, putting aside all emotion, let him apply just a little reason to the problem by counting the true cost of the war and deciding whether the object he seeks to achieve by it is worth that much, even if he were certain of victory, which does not always favor in even the best of causes. "(Erasmus)

"When the prince has made his calculations and reckoned up the total of all these woes (if indeed they could ever be reckoned up), then let him say to himself: 'Shall I alone be the cause of so much woe? Shall so much human blood, so many widows, so many grief-stricken households, so many childless old people, so many made undeservedly poor, the total ruin of morality, law and religion: shall all this be laid at my door? Must I atone for all this before Christ?" (Erasmus)

Questions for Discussion:
1. In debates regarding warfare, how do we be sure to highlight the evils and costs of the proposed conflict?
2. Can we hope to reform a despotic society through warfare?

III. International Agreements

"[Republics] take more time in formulating resolutions, and therefore will less promptly break their faith. Alliances are broken from consideration of interest; and in this respect republics are much more careful in the observance of treaties than princes.." (Machiavelli)

"having all doors closed to him, he was forced to accept what friendships he could find." (Machiavelli)

"It is a truth certain in the law of nature, that he who has made a promise to another, has given to that other a perfect right to demand the performance of the promise. Nations and the representatives of nations, therefore, ought to preserve inviolably their treaties and engagements: by not preserving them, they subject themselves to all the consequences of violating the perfect right of those, to whom they were made. This great truth is generally acknowledged; but too frequently an irreligious disregard is shown to it in the conduct of princes and states. But such a disregard is weak as well as wicked. In publick as in private life, among sovereigns as among individuals, honesty is the best policy, as well as the soundest morality. Among merchants, credit is wealth; among states and princes, good faith is both respectability and power." (Wilson)

Questions for Discussion:
1. How do treaties between nations contribute to peace?
2. Why is it important to maintain diplomatic relations with those nations with whom we

have conflicting interests?

IV. Just War

"The first step the aggressor ought to take, should be an offer of indemnity to the injured party, by the arbitration of some independents and disinterested state. And if this mediation be rejected, then his war assumes the character of a just war." (Grotius)

"...three things are required for a war to be just. Indeed the first requirement us that the ruler at whose command the war is to be waged have the lawful authority to do so...[it] belongs to rulers to use weapons of war to protect the commonwealth against foreign enemies...Second, there needs to be a just cause to wage war, namely that the enemy deserved the war against it because of some wrong it has inflicted....when peoples or political communities need to be punished because they have failed to rectify wrongs committed by their subjects, or because they failed to restore property unjustly seized... Third those waging the war need to have the right intention, namely an intention to promote good or avoid evil. And so Augustine says: "For true worshippers of God, wars waged with zeal for peace and not out of desire for gain or out of cruelty, wars waged to restrain wicked and assist the good, are also conducive of peace...Desire to harm, vengeful cruelty, insatiate and implacable animus, savagery in renewing combat, lust for dominance, and the like are justly condemned in the matter of waging war..." (Aquinas)

"I should have a right to destroy that which threatened me with destruction: for, by the fundamental law of nature, man being to be preserved as much as possible, when all cannot be preserved, the safety of the innocent is to be preferred and one may destroy a man who makes war upon him, or has discovered an enmity to his being, for the same reason that he may kill a wolf or a lion, because such men are not under the ties of the common law of reason, have no other rule, but that of force and violence, and so may be treated as beasts of prey, those dangerous and noxious creatures, that will be sure to destroy him whenever he falls into their power." (Locke)

"...he who would get me into his power, without my consent, would use me as he pleased when he had got

me in his absolute power, unless it be to compel me by force to that which is against the right of my freedom, i.e. makes me a slave. To be free from such force is the only security of my preservation." (Locke)

"The life of governments is like that of man. The latter has a right to kill in case of natural defense; the former have a right to wage war for their own preservation...with states the right of natural defense carries along with it sometime the necessity of attacking; as, for instance, when one nation sees that a continuance of peace will enable another to destroy her, and that to attack that nation instantly is the only way to prevent her own destruction...the right, therefore, of war is derived from necessity and strict justice...when they proceed on principles of glory, convenience, and utility, blood must overspread the earth. But, above all, let them not plead such idle pretext as glory...glory is nothing but pride, it is a passion, and not a legitimate right" (Montesquieu)

"Injury, or the prevention of injury, forms the only justifiable cause of war...all the evil consequences of war are laid at the door of the aggressor." (Grotius)

"The danger must be immediate, which is one necessary point...they are themselves much mistaken and mislead others, who maintain that any degree of fear ought to be a ground for killing another, to prevent his SUPPOSED intention." (Grotius)

"...to maintain a bare probability of some remote, or future annoyance from a neighboring state affords a just ground of hostile aggression, is a doctrine repugnant to every principle of equity. Such, however, is the condition of human life, that no full security can be enjoyed. The only protection against uncertain fears must be sought, not from violence, but from the divine providence, and defensive precaution." (Grotius)

Questions for Discussion:
1. What are just reasons for warfare?
2. How clear and present does a danger have to be in order to justify a preemptive use of force?

V. Defensive Measures

"..whoever has fortified his own town...will be attacked with great reluctance...it can never appear easy to attack one who has his town stoutly defended and is not hated by the people...always keep food, drink and fuel for one year in the public storehouse...a prudent prince will not find it difficult to uphold the courage of his subjects both at the commencement and during a state of siege, if he possesses provisions and means to defend himself..." (Machiavelli)

"...as a guard or against these apprehensions, every power may construct, in its own territory, strong works, and other military securities of the same kind, without having recourse to actual war. One cannot but admire the character which Tacitus has drawn of the Chauci, a noble and high spirited people of Germany, who he says, where desirous of maintaining their greatness by justice, rather than by acts of ungovernable rapacity and ambition—provoking no wars, invading no countries, spoiling no neighbors to aggrandize themselves, yet when necessity prompted, able to raise men with arms in their hands at a moment's warning—a great population with a numerous breed of horses to form a well mounted cavalry—and with all these advantages, upholding their reputation in the midst of peace." (Grotius)

"...be reverently submissive both to good and gentle rulers and those who are overbearing...when many Roman emperors were tyrannically persecuting the Christian faith...the faithful are praised for not resisting and for patiently undergoing death for Christ, although they are equipped to resist...public authority rather than individuals private initiative should take action against the severity of tyrants...if the people should be altogether unable to obtain human help against a tyrant, it should have recourse to the universal king, God, who is a helper in times of oppression and distress...but the people, in order to merit to gain this benefit from God, should stop sinning, since he allows the wicked to rule as a punishment of sin, as the Lord says through Hosea..."I shall in my anger against you give you kings"...therefore we should eliminate sin if we wish to eliminate the scourge of tyrants." (Aquinas)

"..if he yields it from fear, it is for the purpose of avoiding war, and he will rarely escape from that; for he to whom he has from cowardice conceded the one thing will not be satisfied, but will want to take other things from him, and his arrogance will increase as his esteem for the prince is lessened. And on the other hand, the zeal of the prince's friends will be chilled on seeing him appear feeble or cowardly. But, if so soon as he discerns his adversary's intention he prepares his forces, even though they be inferior, the enemy will begin to respect him, and the other neighboring princes will appreciate him the more; and seeing him armed for defense, those even will come to his aid, who, seeing him give up himself, would never have assisted him." (Machiavelli)

Questions for Discussion:
1. What role does national defense play when our ultimate goal is peace?
2. Machiavelli advocates for strong defensive preparation in the face of threats. What are

   the second and third order affects of appeasement to aggression?

VI. Humility in Word

"I hold it to be a proof of great prudence for men to abstain from threats and insulting words towards any one, for neither the one nor the other in any way diminishes the strength of the enemy; but the one makes him more cautious, and the other increases his hatred of you and makes him more persevering in his efforts to injure you." (Machiavelli)

"..so dangerous did the Roman's esteem it to treat men with contempt or reproach them with any previous disgrace, because nothing is more irritating and calculated to excite greater indignation than such reproaches whether founded in truth or not; "for harsh sarcasms, even if they have but the least truth in them, leave their bitterness rankling in the memory." (Machiavelli)

Questions for Discussion:
    1. How can the language our national leaders use inflame or reduce global tensions?

VII. Conduct of War

"Since the purpose of war is the destruction of the enemy state, one has the right to kill the defenders of that state so long as they bear arms. But as soon as they lay down their arms and surrender, they cease to be enemies of instruments of the enemy...war does not grant a right that is unnecessary to its purpose." (Rousseau)

"What general aim the person in power sets himself is of great importance, for if his choice of objective is misguided, then he will necessarily go wrong all the way along." (Erasmus)

"It is a plain case, that when the conquest is completed, the conqueror has no longer a right to kill, because he has no longer the plea of natural defense and self-preservation." (Montesquieu)

"It is a conqueror's business to repair a part of the mischief he has occasioned. The right, therefore, of conquest I define thus: a necessary, lawful, but unhappy power, which leaves the conqueror under a heavy obligation of repairing the injuries done to humanity." (Montesquieu)

"It is your duty then to prosecute the war with all the earnestness in your power. Your glorious prestige must be defended and so must the safety of your allies. You have also got to protect your principal sources of income, and the fortunes of a large number of individual citizens — which cannot be separated from the interests of the state." (Cicero)

"..one ought never to allow a disorder to take place in order to avoid war, for war is not thereby avoided, but only deferred to your disadvantage." (Machiavelli)

"…it is to be noted, that in taking a state the conqueror must arrange to commit all his cruelties at once, so as not to have to recur them every day, and so as to be able, by not making fresh changes, to reassure the people and win them over by benefiting them." (Machiavelli)

"Whoever impoverishes himself by war acquires no power, even though he be victorious, for his conquests cost him more than they are worth." (Machiavelli)

Questions for Discussion:
1. What responsibilities does a nation owe to those it has defeated in war?
2. What are some costs of war?

VIII. Coalition Warfare; Refugees

"..the arms of others either fail, overburden, or else impede you..." (Machiavelli)

"Every one may begin a war at his pleasure, but cannot so finish it. A prince, therefore, before engaging in any enterprise should well measure his strength, and govern himself accordingly; and he must be very careful not to deceive himself in the estimate of his strength, which he will assuredly do if he measures it by his money, or by the situation of his country, or he good disposition of its people, unless he has at the same time an armed force of his own." (Machiavelli)

"We see then how vain the faith and promises of men are who are exiles from their own country. As to their faith, we have to bear in mind that whenever they can return to their country by other means than your assistance, they will abandon you and look to the other means, regardless of their promises to you. And as their vain hopes and promises, such is their extreme desire to return to their homes that they naturally believe many things that are not true, and add many others on purpose, so that with what they really believe and what they say they believe, they will fill you with hopes to that degree that if you attempt to act upon them you will incur a fruitless expense, or engage in an undertaking that will involve you in ruin...A prince therefore should be slow in undertaking any enterprise upon the representation of exiles, for he will generally gain nothing by it but shame and serious injury." (Machiavelli)

Discussion:

1. How should Machievelli's warning "that the arms of others either fail, overburden, or else impede you," inform our involvement in coalition warfare?

2. What about the warning to be careful or exiles? How can refugees and expatriates skew our understanding of the situation on the ground in their home countries?

IX. Peace Treaties

"This is the perfect condition of slavery, which is nothing else, but the state of war continued, between the lawful conqueror and a captive for, if once compact

enter between them, and make an agreement for a limited power on the one side, and obedience on the other, the state of war and slavery ceases, as long as the compact endures for as has been said, no man can, by agreement, pass over to another that which he hath not in himself, a power over his own life." (Locke)

"...without a contract among nations, peace can be neither inaugurated nor guaranteed. A league of a special sort must be established, one that we can call a league of peace, which will be distinguished from a treaty of peace, because the latter seeks merely to stop one war, while the former seeks to end all wars forever...Reason can provide related nations with no other means for emerging from the state of lawlessness, which consists solely of war, than that they give up their savage (lawless) freedom, just as individual persons do, and by accommodating themselves to the constraints of common law, establish a nation of peoples that will finally include all the people of the earth." (Kant)

[Spartans seeking peace] "Indeed if great enmities are ever to be really settled, we think it will not be by the system of revenge and military success, and by forcing an opponent to swear to a treaty to his disadvantage; but when the more fortunate combatant waives his privileges and guided by gentler feelings, conquers his rival in generosity and accords peace on more moderate conditions than expected." (Thucydides)

Questions for Discussion:
1. Why is securing the peace as important as winning the war?
2. Kant's vision of a League of Nations and covenant of peace was realized in the United Nation's charter. Why has the prohibition of all but defensive war not secured the peace as he predicted?

End of Chapter Exercise
1. Consider the conflicts the US has been engaged in over time. Examine the justness of the causes they were fought over. As debates emerge about current and future conflicts, be prepared to advocate for just causes through letters to the editor, engagements with congressional leaders, etc.
2. Members of the US military swear an oath to protect and defend the Constitution of the United States, and to obey the orders of the President of the United States and the officers appointed over them. Regardless of our feelings about the justness of any particular conflict, our nation's military deserve our respect. Determine what you and your family can do to support the troops and do it.
3. Be willing to talk about our civic duty to serve in our nation's armed forces. While the US military is currently and all volunteer

force, quality people throughout the socio-economic spectrum are needed. Not everyone can or should serve, but it is our duty to consider whether it is appropriate for us, and to encourage our children to likewise contemplate such service. No one is "too good" to serve. Unfortunately, too few of the rising generation are qualified to serve, due to issues with fitness, physical and mental health, legal issues, or intellectual aptitude. Shouldn't we want our best and brightest leading such a significant effort and advising our nation's elected leaders?

Chapter 8: On Tyranny

In order to fully appreciate liberty, we must understand tyranny. Despotism begins when the will of man governs, versus the rule of law, and when personal ambition becomes the primary motivator of our leaders. Even in free societies, such temptations exist and must be kept in check.

I. The Nature of Despotism

"…wherever the power that is put in any hands for the government of the people and the preservation of their properties is applied to other ends and made use of to impoverish, harass, or subdue them to the arbitrary and irregular commands of those that have it, there it presently becomes tyranny." (Locke)

"In these [arbitrary] governments, in defiance of religion, humanity, and common sense, millions must be miserable to exalt an embellish one or a few, and to make them proud, arrogant and great: Protection and security are no more, the spirit of the people is sunk, their industry discouraged and lost, or only employed to feed luxury and pride, and multitudes starve, that a few may no riot an abound." (Trenchard)

"It cannot be called virtue to kill one's fellow-citizens, betray one's friends, be without faith, without pity, and without religion; by these methods one may indeed gain power, but not glory." (Machiavelli)

"…[a tyrant's] power will make him still more envious, untrustworthy, unjust, friendless, and godless, a refuge

from every iniquity, and you can see that he's a source of misery above all to himself, but also to his neighbors." (Plato)

"...tyranny is the exercise of power beyond right, which nobody can have a right to, and this is making use of the power any one has in his hands, not for the good of those who are under it, but for his own private separate advantage.   When the governor, however entitled, makes not the law, but his will the rule; and his commands and actions are not directed to the preservation of the properties of his people, but the satisfaction of his own ambition, revenge, covetousness, or any other irregular passion..." (Locke)

"a king governing in a settled kingdom, leaves to be a king, and degenerates into a tyrant, as soon as he leaves off to rule according to his laws…[making] all give way to his own will and appetite." (Locke)

"Their first aim is to break the spirit of their subjects. They know that a poor-spirited man will never plot against anybody. Their second aim is to breed mutual distrust. Tyranny is never overthrown until the people can begin to trust one another and this is the reason why tyrants are always at war with the good…The third and last aim of tyranny is to make their subjects incapable of action. Nobody attempts the impossible." (Aristotle)

"If you get, in public affairs, men whose life is impoverished and destitute of personal satisfactions, but whose hope to snatch some compensation for their own inadequacy from a political career, there can never be good government. They start fighting for power, and the consequent internal and domestic conflicts ruin both them and society." (Plato)

"..I think we shall find when he has disposed of his foreign enemies by treaty or destruction and has no more to fear from them, he will in the first place continue to stir up war in order that the people may continue to need a leader." (Plato)

[Corruption] "Today, because of the profits to be derived from office and the handling of public property, people want to hold office continuously. It is as if they were invalids, who got the benefit of being healthy by being permanently in office…those constitutions which consider the common interest are right constitutions, judged by the standard of absolute justice. Those constitutions which consider only the personal interest of the rulers are all wrong constitutions, or perversions of the right forms. Such perverted forms are despotic, whereas the city is an association of freemen." (Aristotle)

Questions for Discussion:
    1. What are the motives of a despotic ruler?

II. Tyranny in Conquest

"Despotical power is an absolute, arbitrary power one man has over another, to take away his life, whenever he pleases. This is a power, which neither nature gives, for it has made no such distinction between one man over another, nor compact can convey; for man not having such an arbitrary power over his own life, cannot give another man such a power over it; but it is the effect only of forfeiture, which the aggressor makes of his own life, when he puts himself into the state of war with another, for having quitted reason, which God hath given to be the rule betwixt man and man, the common bond whereby human kind is united into fellowship and society; and having renounced the way of peace which that teaches, and made use of the force of war, to compass his unjust ends upon another, where he has no right; and so revolting from his own kind to that of beasts, by making force, which is theirs, to be his rule of right, he renders himself liable to be destroyed by the injured person, and the rest of mankind, that will join with him in the execution of

justice, as any other wild beast, or noxious brute, with whom mankind can have neither society nor security.

And thus captives, taken in a just and lawful war, and such only, are subject to despotical power, which, as it arises not from compact, so neither is it capable of any, but is the state of war continued: for what compact can be made with a man that is not master of his own life? What condition can he perform? And if he be once allowed to be master of his own life, the despotical, arbitrary power of his master ceases. He that is master of himself, and his own life, has a right too to the means of preserving it; so that as soon as compact enters, slavery ceases, and he so far quits his absolute power and puts an end to the state of war who enters into conditions with his captive." (Locke)

"...the conqueror, if he have a just cause, has a despotical right over the persons of all that actually aided and concurred in the war against him, and a right to make up damage and cost out of their labor and estates, so he injure not the right of any other. Over the rest of the people...he has no power and so can have by virtue of conquest, no lawful title himself to dominion over them, or derive it to his posterity; but is an aggressor, if he attempts upon his properties, and thereby puts himself in a state of war against them...nor can such a usurper, or any deriving from him, ever have a title till the people are both at liberty to consent, and have actually consented to allow, and confirm in him the power he hath till then usurped." (Locke)

Questions for Discussion:
1. Will all occupying forces naturally devolve into in tyrannies over time? What changes would be necessary to prevent that?

III. The Evils of Self Interest and Faction in Government

"Avarice, ambition, revenge or gallantry would break the strongest chords of our Constitution...[which] was made only for a moral and religious people. It is wholly inadequate to the government of any other." John Adams

"The cause of all these evils was the lust for power arising from greed and ambition; and from these passions preceded the violence of parties once engaged in contention. The leaders in the cities made the fairest professions: on the one side with the cry of political equality of The People, on the other of a moderate aristocracy; but they sought prizes for themselves in those public interests which the pretended to cherish and, stopping at nothing in their struggles for ascendancy, engaged in direct excesses." (Thucydides)

"By far the warmest advocate of the expedition was, however, Alicibiades…who was…exceedingly ambitious of a command by which he hoped to reduce Sicily and Carthage, and personally to gain in wealth and reputation by means of his success." (Thucydides)

"The most important rule of all…is that provision should be made…to prevent the officials from being able to use their office for their own gain…if the use of profit were made impossible…the poor would no longer desire to hold office (because they would derive no advantage from doing so) and they would prefer to attend to their own affairs. The rich would be able to afford to take office, as they would need no subvention from public funds to meet its expenses. The poor would thus have the advantage of becoming wealthy by diligent attention to work, and notables would enjoy the consolation of not being governed by any chance comer." (Aristotle)

"Where corruption has penetrated a people, the best laws are of no avail, unless they are administered by a man of such supreme power that he may cause the laws to be observed until the mass has been restored to a healthy condition…" (Machiavelli)

"Once public service ceases to be the chief business of the citizens, and they prefer to serve with their wallet rather than with their person, the state is already near its ruin. Is it necessary to march off to battle? They pay mercenary troops and stay at home. Is it necessary to go to the council? They name deputies and stay at home. By dint of laziness and money, they finally have soldiers to enslave the country and representatives to sell it." (Rousseau)

"The man fawning, the servile flatteries, the deceitful correspondences, the base ingratitude to old benefactors, and the slavish compliances with new friends, and all the other arts and treacheries, which are necessary to put into practice in order to rise in such courts, or indeed to become the heads of parties even in free governments, make it almost impossible for a truly great of virtuous man to attain to those stations. A good man will choose to live in an innocent obscurity, and enjoy internal satisfaction resulting from a just sense of his own merit and virtue, rather than aim at greatness, by a long series of unworthy arts and ignoble actions; whilst the ambitious, the cruel, the rapacious, the false, the proud, the treacherous part of mankind will be ever thrusting themselves forward, and endeavoring to sparkle in courts, as well as in the eyes of the unthinking crowds and, to make themselves necessary, will be continually either flattering or distressing princes." (Trenchard)

"…Tyranny had usurped the place of equality, which is the soul of liberty, and destroyed public courage. The minds of men, terrified by unjust power, degenerated into all the vileness and methods of servitude: abject sycophancy and blind submission grew the only means of preferment, and indeed of safety; men durst not open their mouths, but to flatter." (Trenchard)

"Hence grew the necessity of government; which was the mutual contract of a number of men, agreeing upon certain terms of union and society, and putting themselves under penalties, if the violated those terms, which were called laws, and put into the hands of one or men to execute. And thus men quitted part of their natural liberty to acquire civil security. But frequently the remedy proved worse than the disease; and human society had often no enemies so great as their own magistrates; who, wherever they were trusted with too much power, always abused it, and grew mischievous to those who made them what they were." (Trenchard)

"...Power, without control, appertains to God alone; and no man ought to be trusted with what no man is equal to. In truth, there are so many passions and inconsistencies, and so much selfishness belonging to human nature, that we can scarce be too much upon our guard against each other. The only security that we can have that men will be honest, is to make it their interests to be honest; and the best defense which we can have against their being knaves, is to make it terrible to them to be knaves." (Trenchard)

Questions for Discussion:
1. What is the link between corruption and tyranny?

End of Chapter Exercise:
Consider how corruption and avarice can derail liberty even in a free society. What danger exists if this remains unchecked? Make a list of evidences you have seen of these lesser forms of tyranny in society. Determine what you can do to combat it, and do it.

Appendix A

Virginia Declaration of Rights
(George Mason)

A DECLARATION OF RIGHTS made by the representatives of the good people of Virginia, assembled in full and free convention which rights do pertain to them and their posterity, as the basis and foundation of government .

Section 1. That all men are by nature equally free and independent and have certain inherent rights, of which, when they enter into a state of society, they cannot, by any compact, deprive or divest their posterity; namely, the enjoyment of life and liberty, with the means of acquiring and possessing property, and pursuing and obtaining happiness and safety.

Section 2. That all power is vested in, and consequently derived from, the people; that magistrates are their trustees and servants and at all times amenable to them.

Section 3. That government is, or ought to be, instituted for the common benefit, protection, and security of the people, nation, or community; of all the various modes and forms of government, that is best which is capable of producing the greatest degree of happiness and safety and is most effectually secured against the danger of maladministration. And that, when any government shall be found inadequate or contrary to these purposes, a majority of the community has an indubitable, inalienable, and indefeasible right to reform, alter, or abolish it, in such manner as shall be judged most conducive to the public weal.

Section 4. That no man, or set of men, is entitled to exclusive or separate emoluments or privileges from the community, but in consideration of public services; which, nor being descendible, neither ought the offices of magistrate, legislator, or judge to be hereditary.

Section 5. That the legislative and executive powers of the state should be separate and distinct from the judiciary; and that the members of the two first may be restrained from oppression, by feeling and participating the burdens of the people, they should, at fixed periods, be reduced to a private station, return into that body from which they were originally taken, and the vacancies be supplied by frequent, certain, and regular elections, in which all, or any part, of the former members, to be again eligible, or ineligible, as the laws shall direct.

Section 6. That elections of members to serve as representatives of the people, in assembly ought to be free; and that all men, having sufficient evidence of permanent common interest with, and attachment to, the community, have the right of suffrage and cannot be taxed or deprived of their property for public uses without their own consent or that of their representatives so elected, nor bound by any law to which they have not, in like manner, assembled for the public good.

Section 7. That all power of suspending laws, or the execution of laws, by any authority, without consent of the representatives of the people, is injurious to their rights and ought not to be exercised.

Section 8. That in all capital or criminal prosecutions a man has a right to demand the cause and nature of his accusation, to be confronted with the accusers and witnesses, to call for evidence in his favor, and to a speedy trial by an impartial jury of twelve men of his vicinage, without whose unanimous consent he cannot be found guilty; nor can he be compelled to give evidence against himself; that no man be deprived of his liberty except by the law of the land or the judgment of his peers.

Section 9. That excessive bail ought not to be required, nor excessive fines imposed, nor cruel and unusual punishments inflicted.

Section 10. That general warrants, whereby an officer or messenger may be commanded to search suspected places without evidence of a fact committed, or to seize any person or persons not named, or whose offense is not particularly described and supported by evidence, are grievous and oppressive and ought not to be granted.

Section 11. That in controversies respecting property, and in suits between man and man, the ancient trial by jury is preferable to any other and ought to be held sacred.

Section 12. That the freedom of the press is one of the great bulwarks of liberty, and can never be restrained but by despotic governments.

Section 13. That a well-regulated militia, composed of the body of the people, trained to arms, is the proper, natural, and safe defense of a free state; that standing armies, in time of peace, should be avoided as dangerous to liberty; and that in all cases the military should be under strict subordination to, and governed by, the civil power.

Section 14. That the people have a right to uniform government; and, therefore, that no government separate from or independent of the government of Virginia ought to be erected or established within the limits thereof.

Section 15. That no free government, or the blessings of liberty, can be preserved to any people but by a firm adherence to justice, moderation, temperance, frugality, and virtue and by frequent recurrence to fundamental principles.

Section 16. That religion, or the duty which we owe to our Creator, and the manner of discharging it, can be directed only by reason and conviction, not by force or violence; and therefore all men are equally entitled to the free exercise of religion, according to the dictates of conscience; and that it is the mutual duty of all to practise Christian forbearance, love, and charity toward each other.

Appendix B

Constitution of the United States

The Constitution of the United States

Preamble

We the People of the United States, in Order to form a more perfect Union, establish Justice, insure domestic Tranquility, provide for the common defence, promote the general Welfare, and secure the Blessings of Liberty to ourselves and our Posterity, do ordain and establish this Constitution for the United States of America.

Article I - The Legislative Branch Note

Section 1 - The Legislature

All legislative Powers herein granted shall be vested in a Congress of the United States, which shall consist of a Senate and House of Representatives.

Section 2 - The House

The House of Representatives shall be composed of Members chosen every second Year by the People of the several States, and the Electors in each State shall have the Qualifications requisite for Electors of the most numerous Branch of the State Legislature.

No Person shall be a Representative who shall not have attained to the Age of twenty five Years, and been seven Years a Citizen of the United States, and who shall not, when elected, be an Inhabitant of that State in which he shall be chosen.

(Representatives and direct Taxes shall be apportioned among the several States which may be included within this Union, according to their respective Numbers, which shall be determined by adding to the whole Number of free Persons, including those bound to Service for a Term of Years, and excluding Indians not taxed, three fifths of all other Persons.) (The previous sentence in parentheses was modified by the 14th Amendment, section 2.) The actual Enumeration shall be made within three Years after the first Meeting of the Congress of the United States, and within every subsequent Term of ten Years, in such Manner as they shall by Law direct. The Number of Representatives shall not exceed one for every thirty Thousand, but each State shall have at Least one Representative; and until such enumeration shall be made, the State of New Hampshire shall be entitled to chuse three, Massachusetts eight, Rhode Island and Providence Plantations one, Connecticut five, New York six, New Jersey four, Pennsylvania eight, Delaware one, Maryland six, Virginia ten, North Carolina five, South Carolina five and Georgia three.

When vacancies happen in the Representation from any State, the Executive Authority thereof shall issue Writs of Election to fill such Vacancies.

The House of Representatives shall chuse their Speaker and other Officers; and shall have the sole Power of Impeachment.

Section 3 - The Senate

The Senate of the United States shall be composed of two Senators from each State, (chosen by the Legislature thereof,) (The preceding words in parentheses superseded by 17th Amendment, section 1.) for six Years; and each Senator shall have one Vote. Immediately after they shall be assembled in Consequence of the first Election, they shall be divided as equally as may be into three Classes. The Seats of the Senators of the first Class shall be vacated at the Expiration of the second Year, of the second Class at the Expiration of the fourth Year, and of the third Class at the Expiration of the sixth Year, so that one third may be chosen every second Year; (and if Vacancies happen by Resignation, or otherwise, during the Recess of the Legislature of any State, the Executive thereof may make temporary Appointments until the next Meeting of the Legislature, which shall then fill such Vacancies.) (The preceding words in parentheses were superseded by the 17th Amendment, section 2.)

No person shall be a Senator who shall not have attained to the Age of thirty Years, and been nine Years a Citizen of the United States, and who shall not, when elected, be an Inhabitant of that State for which he shall be chosen.

The Vice President of the United States shall be President of the Senate, but shall have no Vote, unless they be equally divided.

The Senate shall chuse their other Officers, and also a President pro tempore, in the absence of the Vice President, or when he shall exercise the Office of President of the United States.

The Senate shall have the sole Power to try all Impeachments. When sitting for that Purpose, they shall be on Oath or Affirmation. When the President of the United States is tried, the Chief Justice shall preside: And no Person shall be convicted without the Concurrence of two thirds of the Members present.
Judgment in Cases of Impeachment shall not extend further than to removal from Office, and disqualification to hold and enjoy any Office of honor, Trust or Profit under the United States: but the Party convicted shall nevertheless be liable and subject to Indictment, Trial, Judgment and Punishment, according to Law.

Section 4 - Elections, Meetings

The Times, Places and Manner of holding Elections for Senators and Representatives, shall be prescribed in each State by the Legislature thereof; but the Congress may at any time by Law make or alter such Regulations, except as to the Place of Chusing Senators.

The Congress shall assemble at least once in every Year, and such Meeting shall (be on the first Monday in December,) (The preceding words in parentheses were superseded by the 20th Amendment, section 2.) unless they shall by Law appoint a different Day.

Section 5 - Membership, Rules, Journals, Adjournment
Each House shall be the Judge of the Elections, Returns and Qualifications of its own Members, and a Majority of each shall constitute a Quorum to do Business; but a smaller number may adjourn from day to day, and may be authorized to compel the Attendance of absent Members, in such Manner, and under such Penalties as each House may provide.

Each House may determine the Rules of its Proceedings, punish its Members for disorderly Behavior, and, with the Concurrence of two-thirds, expel a Member.

Each House shall keep a Journal of its Proceedings, and from time to time publish the same, excepting such Parts as may in their Judgment require Secrecy; and the Yeas and Nays of the Members of either House on any question shall, at the Desire of one fifth of those Present, be entered on the Journal.

Neither House, during the Session of Congress, shall, without the Consent of the other, adjourn for more than three days, nor to any other Place than that in which the two Houses shall be sitting.

Section 6 - Compensation

(The Senators and Representatives shall receive a Compensation for their Services, to be ascertained by Law, and paid out of the Treasury of the United States.) (The preceding words in parentheses were modified by the 27th Amendment.) They shall in all Cases, except Treason, Felony and Breach of the Peace, be privileged from Arrest during their Attendance at the Session of their respective Houses, and in going to and returning from the same; and for any Speech or Debate in either House, they shall not be questioned in any other Place.
No Senator or Representative shall, during the Time for which he was elected, be appointed to any civil Office under the Authority of the United States which shall have been created, or the Emoluments whereof shall have been increased during such time; and no Person holding any Office under the United States, shall be a Member of either House during his Continuance in Office.

Section 7 - Revenue Bills, Legislative Process, Presidential Veto

All bills for raising Revenue shall originate in the House of Representatives; but the Senate may propose or concur with Amendments as on other Bills. Every Bill which shall have passed the House of Representatives and the Senate, shall, before it become a Law, be presented to the President of the United States; If he approve he shall sign it, but if not he shall return it, with his Objections to that House in which it shall have originated, who shall enter the Objections at large on their Journal, and proceed to reconsider it. If after such Reconsideration two thirds of that House shall agree to pass the Bill, it shall be sent, together with the Objections, to the other House, by which it shall likewise be reconsidered, and if approved by two thirds of that House, it shall become a Law. But in all such Cases the Votes of both Houses shall be determined by Yeas and Nays, and the Names of the Persons voting for and against the Bill shall be entered on the Journal of each House respectively. If any Bill shall not be returned by the President within ten Days (Sundays excepted) after it shall have been presented to him, the Same shall be a Law, in like Manner as if he had signed it, unless the Congress by their Adjournment prevent its Return, in which Case it shall not be a Law.

Every Order, Resolution, or Vote to which the Concurrence of the Senate and House of Representatives may be necessary (except on a question of Adjournment) shall be presented to the President of the United States; and before the Same shall take Effect, shall be approved by him, or being disapproved by him, shall be repassed by two thirds of the Senate and House of Representatives, according to the Rules and Limitations prescribed in the Case of a Bill.

Section 8 - Powers of Congress

The Congress shall have Power To lay and collect Taxes, Duties, Imposts and Excises, to pay the Debts and provide for the common Defence and general

Welfare of the United States; but all Duties, Imposts and Excises shall be uniform throughout the United States;

To borrow money on the credit of the United States;

To regulate Commerce with foreign Nations, and among the several States, and with the Indian Tribes;

To establish an uniform Rule of Naturalization, and uniform Laws on the subject of Bankruptcies throughout the United States;

To coin Money, regulate the Value thereof, and of foreign Coin, and fix the Standard of Weights and Measures;

To provide for the Punishment of counterfeiting the Securities and current Coin of the United States;

To establish Post Offices and Post Roads;

To promote the Progress of Science and useful Arts, by securing for limited Times to Authors and Inventors the exclusive Right to their respective Writings and Discoveries;

To constitute Tribunals inferior to the supreme Court;

To define and punish Piracies and Felonies committed on the high Seas, and Offenses against the Law of Nations;

To declare War, grant Letters of Marque and Reprisal, and make Rules concerning Captures on Land and Water;

To raise and support Armies, but no Appropriation of Money to that Use shall be for a longer Term than two Years;

To provide and maintain a Navy;

To make Rules for the Government and Regulation of the land and naval Forces;

To provide for calling forth the Militia to execute the Laws of the Union, suppress Insurrections and repel Invasions;

To provide for organizing, arming, and disciplining, the Militia, and for governing such Part of them as may be employed in the Service of the United States, reserving to the States respectively, the Appointment of the Officers, and the Authority of training the Militia according to the discipline prescribed by Congress;

To exercise exclusive Legislation in all Cases whatsoever, over such District (not exceeding ten Miles square) as may, by Cession of particular States, and the acceptance of Congress, become the Seat of the Government of the United States, and to exercise like Authority over all Places purchased by the Consent of the Legislature of the State in which the Same shall be, for the Erection of Forts, Magazines, Arsenals, dock-Yards, and other needful Buildings; And

To make all Laws which shall be necessary and proper for carrying into Execution the foregoing Powers, and all other Powers vested by this Constitution in the Government of the United States, or in any Department or Officer thereof.

Section 9 - Limits on Congress

The Migration or Importation of such Persons as any of the States now existing shall think proper to admit, shall not be prohibited by the Congress prior to the Year one thousand eight hundred and eight, but a tax or duty may be imposed on such Importation, not exceeding ten dollars for each Person.

The privilege of the Writ of Habeas Corpus shall not be suspended, unless when in Cases of Rebellion or Invasion the public Safety may require it.

No Bill of Attainder or ex post facto Law shall be passed.

(No capitation, or other direct, Tax shall be laid, unless in Proportion to the Census or Enumeration herein before directed to be taken.) (Section in parentheses clarified by the 16th Amendment.)

No Tax or Duty shall be laid on Articles exported from any State.

No Preference shall be given by any Regulation of Commerce or Revenue to the Ports of one State over those of another: nor shall Vessels bound to, or from, one State, be obliged to enter, clear, or pay Duties in another.

No Money shall be drawn from the Treasury, but in Consequence of Appropriations made by Law; and a regular Statement and Account of the Receipts and Expenditures of all public Money shall be published from time to time.

No Title of Nobility shall be granted by the United States: And no Person holding any Office of Profit or Trust under them, shall, without the Consent of the Congress, accept of any present, Emolument, Office, or Title, of any kind whatever, from any King, Prince or foreign State.

Section 10 - Powers prohibited of States

No State shall enter into any Treaty, Alliance, or Confederation; grant Letters of Marque and Reprisal; coin Money; emit Bills of Credit; make any Thing but gold and silver Coin a Tender in Payment of Debts; pass any Bill of Attainder, ex post facto Law, or Law impairing the Obligation of Contracts, or grant any Title of Nobility.

No State shall, without the Consent of the Congress, lay any Imposts or Duties on Imports or Exports, except what may be absolutely necessary for executing it's inspection Laws: and the net Produce of all Duties and Imposts, laid by any State on Imports or Exports, shall be for the Use of the Treasury of the United States; and all such Laws shall be subject to the Revision and Controul of the Congress.

No State shall, without the Consent of Congress, lay any duty of Tonnage, keep Troops, or Ships of War in time of Peace, enter into any Agreement or Compact with another State, or with a foreign Power, or engage in War, unless actually invaded, or in such imminent Danger as will not admit of delay.

Article II - The Executive Branch

Section 1 - The President

The executive Power shall be vested in a President of the United States of America. He shall hold his Office during the Term of four Years, and, together with the Vice-President chosen for the same Term, be elected, as follows:

Each State shall appoint, in such Manner as the Legislature thereof may direct, a Number of Electors, equal to the whole Number of Senators and Representatives to which the State may be entitled in the Congress: but no Senator or Representative, or Person holding an Office of Trust or Profit under the United States, shall be appointed an Elector.

(The Electors shall meet in their respective States, and vote by Ballot for two persons, of whom one at least shall not lie an Inhabitant of the same State with themselves. And they shall make a List of all the Persons voted for, and of the Number of Votes for each; which List they shall sign and certify, and transmit sealed to the Seat of the Government of the United States, directed to the President of the Senate. The President of the Senate shall, in the Presence of the Senate and House of Representatives, open all the Certificates, and the Votes shall then be counted. The Person having the greatest Number of Votes shall be the President, if such Number be a Majority of the whole Number of Electors appointed; and if there be more than one who have such Majority, and have an equal Number of Votes, then the House of Representatives shall immediately chuse by Ballot one of them for President; and if no Person have a Majority, then from the five highest on the List the said House shall in like Manner chuse the President. But in chusing the President, the Votes shall be taken by States, the Representation from each State having one Vote; a quorum for this Purpose shall consist of a Member or Members from two-thirds of the States, and a Majority of all the States shall be necessary to a Choice. In every Case, after the Choice of the President, the Person having the greatest Number of Votes of the Electors shall be the Vice President. But if there should remain two or more who have equal Votes, the Senate shall chuse from them by Ballot the Vice-President.) (This clause in parentheses was superseded by the 12th Amendment.)

The Congress may determine the Time of chusing the Electors, and the Day on which they shall give their Votes; which Day shall be the same throughout the United States.

No person except a natural born Citizen, or a Citizen of the United States, at the time of the Adoption of this Constitution, shall be eligible to the Office of President; neither shall any Person be eligible to that Office who shall not have attained to the Age of thirty-five Years, and been fourteen Years a Resident within the United States.

(In Case of the Removal of the President from Office, or of his Death, Resignation, or Inability to discharge the Powers and Duties of the said Office, the same shall devolve on the Vice President, and the Congress may by Law provide for the Case of Removal, Death, Resignation or Inability, both of the President and Vice President, declaring what Officer shall then act as President, and such Officer shall act accordingly, until the Disability be removed, or a President shall be elected.) (This clause in parentheses has been modified by the 20th and 25th Amendments.)

The President shall, at stated Times, receive for his Services, a Compensation, which shall neither be increased nor diminished during the Period for which he shall have been elected, and he shall not receive within that Period any other Emolument from the United States, or any of them.

Before he enter on the Execution of his Office, he shall take the following Oath or Affirmation:

"I do solemnly swear (or affirm) that I will faithfully execute the Office of President of the United States, and will to the best of my Ability, preserve, protect and defend the Constitution of the United States."

Section 2 - Civilian Power over Military, Cabinet, Pardon Power, Appointments

The President shall be Commander in Chief of the Army and Navy of the United States, and of the Militia of the several States, when called into the actual Service of the United States; he may require the Opinion, in writing, of the principal Officer in each of the executive Departments, upon any subject relating to the Duties of their respective Offices, and he shall have Power to Grant Reprieves and Pardons for Offenses against the United States, except in Cases of Impeachment.

He shall have Power, by and with the Advice and Consent of the Senate, to make Treaties, provided two thirds of the Senators present concur; and he shall nominate, and by and with the Advice and Consent of the Senate, shall appoint Ambassadors, other public Ministers and Consuls, Judges of the supreme Court, and all other Officers of the United States, whose Appointments are not herein otherwise provided for, and which shall be established by Law: but the Congress may by Law vest the Appointment of such inferior Officers, as they think proper, in the President alone, in the Courts of Law, or in the Heads of Departments.

The President shall have Power to fill up all Vacancies that may happen during the Recess of the Senate, by granting Commissions which shall expire at the End of their next Session.

Section 3 - State of the Union, Convening Congress

He shall from time to time give to the Congress Information of the State of the Union, and recommend to their Consideration such Measures as he shall judge necessary and expedient; he may, on extraordinary Occasions, convene both Houses, or either of them, and in Case of Disagreement between them, with Respect to the Time of Adjournment, he may adjourn them to such Time as he shall think proper; he shall receive Ambassadors and other public Ministers; he shall take Care that the Laws be faithfully executed, and shall Commission all the Officers of the United States.

Section 4 - Disqualification

The President, Vice President and all civil Officers of the United States, shall be removed from Office on Impeachment for, and Conviction of, Treason, Bribery, or other high Crimes and Misdemeanors.

Article III - The Judicial Branch Note

Section 1 - Judicial powers

The judicial Power of the United States, shall be vested in one supreme Court, and in such inferior Courts as the Congress may from time to time ordain and establish. The Judges, both of the supreme and inferior Courts, shall hold their Offices during good Behavior, and shall, at stated Times, receive for their Services a Compensation which shall not be diminished during their Continuance in Office.

Section 2 - Trial by Jury, Original Jurisdiction, Jury Trials

(The judicial Power shall extend to all Cases, in Law and Equity, arising under this Constitution, the Laws of the United States, and Treaties made, or which shall be made, under their Authority; to all Cases affecting Ambassadors, other public Ministers and Consuls; to all Cases of admiralty and maritime Jurisdiction; to Controversies to which the United States shall be a Party; to Controversies between two or more States; between a State and Citizens of another State; between Citizens of different States; between Citizens of the same State claiming Lands under Grants of different States, and between a State, or the Citizens thereof, and foreign States, Citizens or Subjects.) (This section in parentheses is modified by the 11th Amendment.)

In all Cases affecting Ambassadors, other public Ministers and Consuls, and those in which a State shall be Party, the supreme Court shall have original Jurisdiction. In all the other Cases before mentioned, the supreme Court shall have appellate Jurisdiction, both as to Law and Fact, with such Exceptions, and under such Regulations as the Congress shall make.

The Trial of all Crimes, except in Cases of Impeachment, shall be by Jury; and such Trial shall be held in the State where the said Crimes shall have been committed; but when not committed within any State, the Trial shall be at such Place or Places as the Congress may by Law have directed.

Section 3 - Treason Note

Treason against the United States, shall consist only in levying War against them, or in adhering to their Enemies, giving them Aid and Comfort. No Person shall be convicted of Treason unless on the Testimony of two Witnesses to the same overt Act, or on Confession in open Court.

The Congress shall have power to declare the Punishment of Treason, but no Attainder of Treason shall work Corruption of Blood, or Forfeiture except during the Life of the Person attainted.

Article IV - The States

Section 1 - Each State to Honor all others

Full Faith and Credit shall be given in each State to the public Acts, Records, and judicial Proceedings of every other State. And the Congress may by general Laws prescribe the Manner in which such Acts, Records and Proceedings shall be proved, and the Effect thereof.

Section 2 - State citizens, Extradition

The Citizens of each State shall be entitled to all Privileges and Immunities of Citizens in the several States.

A Person charged in any State with Treason, Felony, or other Crime, who shall flee from Justice, and be found in another State, shall on demand of the executive Authority of the State from which he fled, be delivered up, to be removed to the State having Jurisdiction of the Crime.

(No Person held to Service or Labour in one State, under the Laws thereof, escaping into another, shall, in Consequence of any Law or Regulation therein, be discharged from such Service or Labour, But shall be delivered up on Claim of the Party to whom such Service or Labour may be due.) (This clause in parentheses is superseded by the 13th Amendment.)

Section 3 - New States

New States may be admitted by the Congress into this Union; but no new States shall be formed or erected within the Jurisdiction of any other State; nor any State be formed by the Junction of two or more States, or parts of States, without the Consent of the Legislatures of the States concerned as well as of the Congress.

The Congress shall have Power to dispose of and make all needful Rules and Regulations respecting the Territory or other Property belonging to the United

States; and nothing in this Constitution shall be so construed as to Prejudice any Claims of the United States, or of any particular State.

Section 4 - Republican government

The United States shall guarantee to every State in this Union a Republican Form of Government, and shall protect each of them against Invasion; and on Application of the Legislature, or of the Executive (when the Legislature cannot be convened) against domestic Violence.

Article V - Amendment

The Congress, whenever two thirds of both Houses shall deem it necessary, shall propose Amendments to this Constitution, or, on the Application of the Legislatures of two thirds of the several States, shall call a Convention for proposing Amendments, which, in either Case, shall be valid to all Intents and Purposes, as part of this Constitution, when ratified by the Legislatures of three fourths of the several States, or by Conventions in three fourths thereof, as the one or the other Mode of Ratification may be proposed by the Congress; Provided that no Amendment which may be made prior to the Year One thousand eight hundred and eight shall in any Manner affect the first and fourth Clauses in the Ninth Section of the first Article; and that no State, without its Consent, shall be deprived of its equal Suffrage in the Senate.

Article VI - Debts, Supremacy, Oaths

All Debts contracted and Engagements entered into, before the Adoption of this Constitution, shall be as valid against the United States under this Constitution, as under the Confederation.

This Constitution, and the Laws of the United States which shall be made in Pursuance thereof; and all Treaties made, or which shall be made, under the Authority of the United States, shall be the supreme Law of the Land; and the Judges in every State shall be bound thereby, any Thing in the Constitution or Laws of any State to the Contrary notwithstanding.

The Senators and Representatives before mentioned, and the Members of the several State Legislatures, and all executive and judicial Officers, both of the United States and of the several States, shall be bound by Oath or Affirmation, to support this Constitution; but no religious Test shall ever be required as a Qualification to any Office or public Trust under the United States.

Article VII - Ratification Documents

The Ratification of the Conventions of nine States, shall be sufficient for the Establishment of this Constitution between the States so ratifying the Same.

Done in Convention by the Unanimous Consent of the States present the Seventeenth Day of September in the Year of our Lord one thousand seven hundred and Eighty seven and of the Independence of the United States of America the Twelfth. In Witness whereof We have hereunto subscribed our Names. Note

Go Washington - President and deputy from Virginia
New Hampshire - John Langdon, Nicholas Gilman
Massachusetts - Nathaniel Gorham, Rufus King
Connecticut - Wm Saml Johnson, Roger Sherman
New York - Alexander Hamilton
New Jersey - Wil Livingston, David Brearley, Wm Paterson, Jona. Dayton
Pensylvania - B Franklin, Thomas Mifflin, Robt Morris, Geo. Clymer, Thos FitzSimons, Jared Ingersoll, James Wilson, Gouv Morris
Delaware - Geo. Read, Gunning Bedford jun, John Dickinson, Richard Bassett, Jaco. Broom
Maryland - James McHenry, Dan of St Tho Jenifer, Danl Carroll
Virginia - John Blair, James Madison Jr.
North Carolina - Wm Blount, Richd Dobbs Spaight, Hu Williamson
South Carolina - J. Rutledge, Charles Cotesworth Pinckney, Charles Pinckney, Pierce Butler
Georgia - William Few, Abr Baldwin
Attest: William Jackson, Secretary

The Amendments

Amendment 1 - Freedom of Religion, Press, Expression. Ratified 12/15/1791.

Congress shall make no law respecting an establishment of religion, or prohibiting the free exercise thereof; or abridging the freedom of speech, or of the press; or the right of the people peaceably to assemble, and to petition the Government for a redress of grievances.

Amendment 2 - Right to Bear Arms. Ratified 12/15/1791.

A well regulated Militia, being necessary to the security of a free State, the right of the people to keep and bear Arms, shall not be infringed.

Amendment 3 - Quartering of Soldiers. Ratified 12/15/1791.

No Soldier shall, in time of peace be quartered in any house, without the consent of the Owner, nor in time of war, but in a manner to be prescribed by law.

Amendment 4 - Search and Seizure. Ratified 12/15/1791.

The right of the people to be secure in their persons, houses, papers, and effects, against unreasonable searches and seizures, shall not be violated, and no Warrants shall issue, but upon probable cause, supported by Oath or affirmation, and particularly describing the place to be searched, and the persons or things to be seized.

Amendment 5 - Trial and Punishment, Compensation for Takings. Ratified 12/15/1791.

No person shall be held to answer for a capital, or otherwise infamous crime, unless on a presentment or indictment of a Grand Jury, except in cases arising in the land or naval forces, or in the Militia, when in actual service in time of War or public danger; nor shall any person be subject for the same offense to be twice put in jeopardy of life or limb; nor shall be compelled in any criminal case to be a witness against himself, nor be deprived of life, liberty, or property, without due process of law; nor shall private property be taken for public use, without just compensation.

Amendment 6 - Right to Speedy Trial, Confrontation of Witnesses. Ratified 12/15/1791.

In all criminal prosecutions, the accused shall enjoy the right to a speedy and public trial, by an impartial jury of the State and district wherein the crime shall have been committed, which district shall have been previously ascertained by law, and to be informed of the nature and cause of the accusation; to be confronted with the witnesses against him; to have compulsory process for obtaining witnesses in his favor, and to have the Assistance of Counsel for his defence.

Amendment 7 - Trial by Jury in Civil Cases. Ratified 12/15/1791.

In Suits at common law, where the value in controversy shall exceed twenty dollars, the right of trial by jury shall be preserved, and no fact tried by a jury, shall be otherwise re-examined in any Court of the United States, than according to the rules of the common law.

Amendment 8 - Cruel and Unusual Punishment. Ratified 12/15/1791.

Excessive bail shall not be required, nor excessive fines imposed, nor cruel and unusual punishments inflicted.

Amendment 9 - Construction of Constitution. Ratified 12/15/1791.

The enumeration in the Constitution, of certain rights, shall not be construed to deny or disparage others retained by the people.

Amendment 10 - Powers of the States and People. Ratified 12/15/1791. Note

The powers not delegated to the United States by the Constitution, nor prohibited by it to the States, are reserved to the States respectively, or to the people.

Amendment 11 - Judicial Limits. Ratified 2/7/1795.

The Judicial power of the United States shall not be construed to extend to any suit in law or equity, commenced or prosecuted against one of the United States by Citizens of another State, or by Citizens or Subjects of any Foreign State.

Amendment 12 - Choosing the President, Vice-President. Ratified 6/15/1804.

The Electors shall meet in their respective states, and vote by ballot for President and Vice-President, one of whom, at least, shall not be an inhabitant of the same state with themselves; they shall name in their ballots the person voted for as President, and in distinct ballots the person voted for as Vice-President, and they shall make distinct lists of all persons voted for as President, and of all persons voted for as Vice-President and of the number of votes for each, which lists they shall sign and certify, and transmit sealed to the seat of the government of the United States, directed to the President of the Senate;

The President of the Senate shall, in the presence of the Senate and House of Representatives, open all the certificates and the votes shall then be counted;
The person having the greatest Number of votes for President, shall be the President, if such number be a majority of the whole number of Electors appointed; and if no person have such majority, then from the persons having the highest numbers not exceeding three on the list of those voted for as President, the House of Representatives shall choose immediately, by ballot, the President. But in choosing the President, the votes shall be taken by states, the representation from each state having one vote; a quorum for this purpose

shall consist of a member or members from two-thirds of the states, and a majority of all the states shall be necessary to a choice. And if the House of Representatives shall not choose a President whenever the right of choice shall devolve upon them, before the fourth day of March next following, then the Vice-President shall act as President, as in the case of the death or other constitutional disability of the President. The person having the greatest number of votes as Vice-President, shall be the Vice-President, if such number be a majority of the whole number of Electors appointed, and if no person have a majority, then from the two highest numbers on the list, the Senate shall choose the Vice-President; a quorum for the purpose shall consist of two-thirds of the whole number of Senators, and a majority of the whole number shall be necessary to a choice. But no person constitutionally ineligible to the office of President shall be eligible to that of Vice-President of the United States.

Amendment 13 - Slavery Abolished. Ratified 12/6/1865.

1. Neither slavery nor involuntary servitude, except as a punishment for crime whereof the party shall have been duly convicted, shall exist within the United States, or any place subject to their jurisdiction.

2. Congress shall have power to enforce this article by appropriate legislation.

Amendment 14 - Citizenship Rights. Ratified 7/9/1868.

1. All persons born or naturalized in the United States, and subject to the jurisdiction thereof, are citizens of the United States and of the State wherein they reside. No State shall make or enforce any law which shall abridge the privileges or immunities of citizens of the United States; nor shall any State deprive any person of life, liberty, or property, without due process of law; nor deny to any person within its jurisdiction the equal protection of the laws.

2. Representatives shall be apportioned among the several States according to their respective numbers, counting the whole number of persons in each State, excluding Indians not taxed. But when the right to vote at any election for the choice of electors for President and Vice-President of the United States, Representatives in Congress, the Executive and Judicial officers of a State, or the members of the Legislature thereof, is denied to any of the male inhabitants of such State, being twenty-one years of age, and citizens of the United States, or in any way abridged, except for participation in rebellion, or other crime, the basis of representation therein shall be reduced in the proportion which the number of such male citizens shall bear to the whole number of male citizens twenty-one years of age in such State.

3. No person shall be a Senator or Representative in Congress, or elector of President and Vice-President, or hold any office, civil or military, under the United

States, or under any State, who, having previously taken an oath, as a member of Congress, or as an officer of the United States, or as a member of any State legislature, or as an executive or judicial officer of any State, to support the Constitution of the United States, shall have engaged in insurrection or rebellion against the same, or given aid or comfort to the enemies thereof. But Congress may by a vote of two-thirds of each House, remove such disability.

4. The validity of the public debt of the United States, authorized by law, including debts incurred for payment of pensions and bounties for services in suppressing insurrection or rebellion, shall not be questioned. But neither the United States nor any State shall assume or pay any debt or obligation incurred in aid of insurrection or rebellion against the United States, or any claim for the loss or emancipation of any slave; but all such debts, obligations and claims shall be held illegal and void.

5. The Congress shall have power to enforce, by appropriate legislation, the provisions of this article.

Amendment 15 - Race No Bar to Vote. Ratified 2/3/1870.

1. The right of citizens of the United States to vote shall not be denied or abridged by the United States or by any State on account of race, color, or previous condition of servitude.
2. The Congress shall have power to enforce this article by appropriate legislation.

Amendment 16 - Status of Income Tax Clarified. Ratified 2/3/1913.

The Congress shall have power to lay and collect taxes on incomes, from whatever source derived, without apportionment among the several States, and without regard to any census or enumeration.

Amendment 17 - Senators Elected by Popular Vote. Ratified 4/8/1913.

The Senate of the United States shall be composed of two Senators from each State, elected by the people thereof, for six years; and each Senator shall have one vote. The electors in each State shall have the qualifications requisite for electors of the most numerous branch of the State legislatures.

When vacancies happen in the representation of any State in the Senate, the executive authority of such State shall issue writs of election to fill such vacancies: Provided, That the legislature of any State may empower the executive thereof to make temporary appointments until the people fill the vacancies by election as the legislature may direct.

This amendment shall not be so construed as to affect the election or term of any Senator chosen before it becomes valid as part of the Constitution.

Amendment 18 - Liquor Abolished. Ratified 1/16/1919. **Repealed by Amendment** 21, 12/5/1933.

1. After one year from the ratification of this article the manufacture, sale, or transportation of intoxicating liquors within, the importation thereof into, or the exportation thereof from the United States and all territory subject to the jurisdiction thereof for beverage purposes is hereby prohibited.

2. The Congress and the several States shall have concurrent power to enforce this article by appropriate legislation.

3. This article shall be inoperative unless it shall have been ratified as an amendment to the Constitution by the legislatures of the several States, as provided in the Constitution, within seven years from the date of the submission hereof to the States by the Congress.

Amendment 19 - Women's Suffrage. Ratified 8/18/1920.

The right of citizens of the United States to vote shall not be denied or abridged by the United States or by any State on account of sex.
Congress shall have power to enforce this article by appropriate legislation.

Amendment 20 - Presidential, Congressional Terms.
Ratified 1/23/1933.

1. The terms of the President and Vice President shall end at noon on the 20th day of January, and the terms of Senators and Representatives at noon on the 3d day of January, of the years in which such terms would have ended if this article had not been ratified; and the terms of their successors shall then begin.

2. The Congress shall assemble at least once in every year, and such meeting shall begin at noon on the 3d day of January, unless they shall by law appoint a different day.

3. If, at the time fixed for the beginning of the term of the President, the President elect shall have died, the Vice President elect shall become President. If a President shall not have been chosen before the time fixed for the beginning of his term, or if the President elect shall have failed to qualify, then the Vice President elect shall act as President until a President shall have qualified; and the Congress may by law provide for the case wherein neither a President elect nor a Vice President elect shall have qualified, declaring who shall then act as President, or the manner in which one who is to act shall be selected, and such person shall act accordingly until a President or Vice President shall have qualified.

4. The Congress may by law provide for the case of the death of any of the persons from whom the House of Representatives may choose a President whenever the

right of choice shall have devolved upon them, and for the case of the death of any of the persons from whom the Senate may choose a Vice President whenever the right of choice shall have devolved upon them.

5. Sections 1 and 2 shall take effect on the 15th day of October following the ratification of this article.

6. This article shall be inoperative unless it shall have been ratified as an amendment to the Constitution by the legislatures of three-fourths of the several States within seven years from the date of its submission.

Amendment 21 - Amendment 18 Repealed. Ratified 12/5/1933.

1. The eighteenth article of amendment to the Constitution of the United States is hereby repealed.

2. The transportation or importation into any State, Territory, or possession of the United States for delivery or use therein of intoxicating liquors, in violation of the laws thereof, is hereby prohibited.

3. The article shall be inoperative unless it shall have been ratified as an amendment to the Constitution by conventions in the several States, as provided in the Constitution, within seven years from the date of the submission hereof to the States by the Congress.

Amendment 22 - Presidential Term Limits. Ratified 2/27/1951.

1. No person shall be elected to the office of the President more than twice, and no person who has held the office of President, or acted as President, for more than two years of a term to which some other person was elected President shall be elected to the office of the President more than once. But this Article shall not apply to any person holding the office of President, when this Article was proposed by the Congress, and shall not prevent any person who may be holding the office of President, or acting as President, during the term within which this Article becomes operative from holding the office of President or acting as President during the remainder of such term.

2. This article shall be inoperative unless it shall have been ratified as an amendment to the Constitution by the legislatures of three-fourths of the several States within seven years from the date of its submission to the States by the Congress.

Amendment 23 - Presidential Vote for District of Columbia. Ratified 3/29/1961.

1. The District constituting the seat of Government of the United States shall appoint in such manner as the Congress may direct: A number of electors of President and Vice President equal to the whole number of Senators and Representatives in Congress to which the District would be entitled if it were a State, but in no

event more than the least populous State; they shall be in addition to those appointed by the States, but they shall be considered, for the purposes of the election of President and Vice President, to be electors appointed by a State; and they shall meet in the District and perform such duties as provided by the twelfth article of amendment.

2. The Congress shall have power to enforce this article by appropriate legislation.

Amendment 24 - Poll Tax Barred. Ratified 1/23/1964.

1. The right of citizens of the United States to vote in any primary or other election for President or Vice President, for electors for President or Vice President, or for Senator or Representative in Congress, shall not be denied or abridged by the United States or any State by reason of failure to pay any poll tax or other tax.

2. The Congress shall have power to enforce this article by appropriate legislation.

Amendment 25 - Presidential Disability and Succession. Ratified 2/10/1967.

1. In case of the removal of the President from office or of his death or resignation, the Vice President shall become President.

2. Whenever there is a vacancy in the office of the Vice President, the President shall nominate a Vice President

who shall take office upon confirmation by a majority vote of both Houses of Congress.

3. Whenever the President transmits to the President pro tempore of the Senate and the Speaker of the House of Representatives his written declaration that he is unable to discharge the powers and duties of his office, and until he transmits to them a written declaration to the contrary, such powers and duties shall be discharged by the Vice President as Acting President.

4. Whenever the Vice President and a majority of either the principal officers of the executive departments or of such other body as Congress may by law provide, transmit to the President pro tempore of the Senate and the Speaker of the House of Representatives their written declaration that the President is unable to discharge the powers and duties of his office, the Vice President shall immediately assume the powers and duties of the office as Acting President. Thereafter, when the President transmits to the President pro tempore of the Senate and the Speaker of the House of Representatives his written declaration that no inability exists, he shall resume the powers and duties of his office unless the Vice President and a majority of either the principal officers of the executive department or of such other body as Congress may by law provide, transmit within four days to the President pro tempore of the Senate and the Speaker of the House of Representatives their written declaration that the President is unable to discharge the powers and duties of his office. Thereupon Congress shall decide the issue, assembling within forty eight hours for that purpose if

not in session. If the Congress, within twenty one days after receipt of the latter written declaration, or, if Congress is not in session, within twenty one days after Congress is required to assemble, determines by two thirds vote of both Houses that the President is unable to discharge the powers and duties of his office, the Vice President shall continue to discharge the same as Acting President; otherwise, the President shall resume the powers and duties of his office.

Amendment 26 - Voting Age Set to 18 Years. Ratified 7/1/1971.

1. The right of citizens of the United States, who are eighteen years of age or older, to vote shall not be denied or abridged by the United States or by any State on account of age.

2. The Congress shall have power to enforce this article by appropriate legislation.

Amendment 27 - Limiting Changes to Congressional Pay. Ratified 5/7/1992.

No law, varying the compensation for the services of the Senators and Representatives, shall take effect, until an election of Representatives shall have intervened.

www.ingramcontent.com/pod-product-compliance
Lightning Source LLC
Chambersburg PA
CBHW070014300526
45794CB00001B/316